THE STORY OF
GRASS-TRACK RACING
1927-49

THE STORY OF
GRASS-TRACK RACING
1927-49

Robert Bamford & Dave Stallworthy

TEMPUS

First published 2002

PUBLISHED IN THE UNITED KINGDOM BY:

Tempus Publishing Ltd
The Mill, Brimscombe Port
Stroud, Gloucestershire GL5 2QG

PUBLISHED IN THE UNITED STATES OF AMERICA BY:

Tempus Publishing Inc.
2A Cumberland Street
Charleston, SC 29401

Tempus books are available in France, Germany and Belgium
from the following addresses:

Tempus Publishing Group	Tempus Publishing Group
21 Avenue de la République	Gustav-Adolf-Straße 3
37300 Joué-lès-Tours	99084 Erfurt
FRANCE	GERMANY

British Library Cataloguing in Publication Data.
A catalogue record for this book is available from the British Library.

ISBN 0 7524 2406 8

Typesetting and origination by Tempus Publishing.
PRINTED AND BOUND IN GREAT BRITAIN.

CONTENTS

ACKNOWLEDGEMENTS

Both Dave Stallworthy and Robert Bamford would like to acknowledge all the many friends and enthusiasts who have helped with news stories, programmes and photographs, which have greatly augmented this story.

Special thanks are due to Bill Cole, John Jarvis, Bob Light, John Ogden, Geoff Parker and Glynn Shailes.

Dave and Robert would like to apologise in advance, should any of our detective work subsequently prove to be erroneous.

INTRODUCTION

Motorcycle grass-track racing has played a big part in my leisure time since 1965, when I first started watching this sport on a regular basis. So much is written about grass-track racing's sister sport, speedway, and other disciplines, such as road racing and motocross, but I felt the history of grass-track racing would be lost if I didn't write something on the subject.

Over the years, I have collected information on each season of grass-track and am aiming to put the highlights into a yearly format and, eventually, to reach 2002 and beyond. Through research and the help of people like John Ogden, I have been able to put this project together. Then entered Robert Bamford, a speedway author and historian from my old home town of Malmesbury in Wiltshire! Robert has already established a reputation of writing some excellent publications on the sport of speedway and I asked him if he would join me in this project. Using his superb desk-top skills, he has put the icing on the cake, with the end result being this story of grass-track, which covers the years 1927 to 1949.

Before 1927, it is difficult to gather much information, although the first grass-track is generally recognized as the 1923 Cambridgeshire Agricultural Show event, when a reputed 20,000 spectators watched the pioneer race action. Racing on oval circuits, though, can be traced back to at least 1904, when a meeting was staged on a loose surface at Portman Road in Ipswich.

The rise of grass-track racing started after the ACU (Auto Cycle Union) banned all speed events on public roads in April 1925, with the Whit Sunday Bank Holiday meeting of 1927 being the first proper grass-track event. That meeting was organized by the Whitgift Club at a disused golf course near Croydon. In the early years, almost anything went when it came to grass-track racing, and the meeting at Croydon was no exception, for they had no safety ropes and the track was marked out with flags! Also, non-skid devices were used on the wheels, such as lengths of rope or chain fixed around the rim and tyre. Midland collector Noel Clark has an example of a wheel with balls attached, while leather straps and spikes were also used on the tyres until they were banned in 1931. That was the year when the ACU drew up regulations, both for safety and for specific classes. Therefore, the past seventy years has seen the sport governed correctly, either by the aforementioned ACU, or by the AMCA (Amateur Motor-Cycle Association).

Today, the sport mainly features riders racing head-to-head, shoulder-to-shoulder for four laps (sometimes six) around an oval speedway-style circuit, which can vary in length from 300 yards to 900 yards. The machines involved, like speedway, have also become very specialized. However, in the period covered within this volume, the bikes, with the minimum of modifications, could be used for grass-track racing, scrambles or even for road racing. In fact, just like in speedway, many of the pioneer riders would arrive at the racing circuit on their machine, before stripping off such items as lights and number plates etc! After the racing, they would replace everything and then ride home!

Tracks could vary greatly: for instance, in the 1930s and 1940s, mountain-style circuits were popular, and venues like Wroughton, Lilleshall and Rushmere could almost be classed as scrambles courses. I have also found that in some parts of Britain, oval tracks were very popular and more akin to the racing we now know. The Swansea, Evesham, St Austell and Bristol areas all witnessed this style of grass action. A lot of the Southern Centre meetings had oval circuits, however, many of them did incorporate an 's' bend or chicane.

Bob Light, a former top commentator and the author of the first 'Rich Mixture' book, has unearthed some very rare photographs of racing action from the Midlands, including some from the mountain circuits. He has very kindly assisted by allowing me to share these rare pictures with everyone.

'S' bends or chicanes were used on a regular basis, right up to the end of the 1960s. They were not popular with the speedway-style riders; however, the riders with scrambles or motocross experience were more than happy with them. With the sidecars, these types of circuits produced some more exciting moves, using the skills of both the driver and the passenger, as well as slowing down the overall race speeds of course.

I believe it is important to keep the grass-track story alive and regular supporters can read about the nostalgia in other publications. The monthly magazine, *Off Road Review*, includes a grass-track section and, over the years, hundreds of photographs from the past have been published. Another magazine called *Track Racing Review*, edited by John Simcock, includes some historic sections, along with modern text and photographs. The Veteran Grass-track Riders Association newsletter, compiled by Carl and Janet Croucher, includes many articles, news and reviews of riders and events from the mists of time. Add to that the rare photographs that have appeared in books by Gordon Frances and Bob Light, and we are now starting to keep the history of the sport alive.

On the racing front, the big annual nostalgia event is the Western Classic Motor-Cycle Club's 'Days of Glory', which is held in Gloucestershire. It incorporates the British Pre-1975 Grass-track Championships, a past masters parade, the Veteran Grass-track Riders Association reunion, American classic flat track TT grass racing, plus racing for vintage, post-vintage and post-war machines. Most years, former rider Noel Clark brings along a display of machinery, which includes bikes formerly raced by Dick Tolley, Ron Taylor and Bill Bridgett, who were star riders in the 1950s and 1960s.

Also each year, the grass-track section of the Vintage Motor-Cycle Club organizes the National Vintage Grass-track Championships, which are held over a series of rounds throughout different parts of Britain, including North Somerset, Oxfordshire, Kent and Lincolnshire. So, as you can see, there is plenty going on in an effort to keep that history alive. Both Robert and myself hope you enjoy this publication.

Dave Stallworthy,
January 2002

1
GRASS-TRACK RACING
1927

Whit Monday started the sport of grass-track racing on its long road of success, with a meeting on the old Addington golf course near Croydon. This was organized by Croydon and District Motor-Cycle Club, who were also sometimes known as the Whitgift Club. Believe it or not, this first Whitgift meeting actually had no ropes or fences and the course was simply marked out by flags! The oval circuit was just over a mile in length, with a slight gradient and, even in those days, the speeds were impressive, as an average of 40mph could be achieved.

Various races were held over three laps, five laps and twenty laps, with the winners from that historic meeting being: Whitgift Members – S. Taylor (490cc Norton); Sidecar – G. Wright (498cc Scott); 175cc Class – C. Barclay (172cc Francis Barnett); Unlimited Class – Alf Foulds (493cc Sunbeam); Addington Grand Prix – Alf Foulds (493cc Sunbeam).

That initial meeting was soon followed by others. On 18 June, the Hampton Court and District Motor Club organized racing on a quarter-mile track at Hurst Park. The event was held in aid of the local hospital, and this time the circuit was roped off in order to safeguard the spectators! Les Blakeborough, mounted on a 348cc Cotton, did the double by winning the 350cc Class and the 500cc Class, while A. Kilfoyle won the Sidecar event on a 989cc Harley Davidson outfit.

Moving north, the North Manchester Club held a meeting on the outskirts of Manchester, which was watched by around 6,000 spectators. The major winners were Wilf McClure, Oliver Langton and E.O. Spence. The latter, of course, went on to be the legendary promoter of speedway at Belle Vue.

That event was followed by a meeting at Belle Vue Gardens and, looking at old photographs, it could possibly even have been held on the site of what would later become the famous speedway venue. Anyway, at a very wet meeting, Wilf McClure completed a glorious double, winning the 500cc and Unlimited Classes.

Back down south, racing was held by the Bournemouth Gypsy Club, while the Mount circuit, at Poulner near Ringwood, was used for the first time. Later that year, this became known as the Ringwood Club.

Other grass-tracks included Austin Light Car and Motor-Cycle Club at Longbridge, near Birmingham; Swansea and District Motor-Cycle Club, who formed part of a Gymkhana at Clyne Valley Racecourse in Swansea; Enfield and District Motor-Cycle and Light Car Club; Stevenage Motor Club at Chell's Farm in Stevenage; and Nottingham Tornadoes Motor Club, who organized racing at Trent Lane, which later became the home of Nottingham Speedway. Overall, it was a good start to the sport of grass-track racing.

Start-line action from Swansea.

1927 Roll Of Honour

North Manchester Club Grand Prix
Solo – Oliver Langton
Sidecar – E.O. Spence

Whitgift Motor Club Grand Prix
Alf Foulds

Austin Longbridge Silver Cup
J.P. Lloyd

Belle Vue Opening Championships
250cc – A. Firth
500cc – Wilf McClure
Unlimited – Wilf McClure
Sidecar – Harry Langman

2
GRASS-TRACK RACING
1928

The season started with another history-making event at Belle Vue in Manchester, namely the British Open. This was not only the first British Open, but Britain's first floodlit grass-track event, with acetylene flares and a searchlight used to light the track.

Racing on the grass was starting to take off in a big way and club-organized events in 1928 included: St Albans at Sandridge; Witney Concrete Speedway; Berkhamsted and District Motor-Cycle Club at Aylesbury Racecourse; Wolverhampton Motor-Cycle and Car Club at Lilleshall Hall; Macclesfield and District Motor-Cycle Club; Southgate and District Motor-Cycle Club; Oxted, Westerham and Limpsfield Motor-Cycle and Light Car Club; Dunstable and District Automobile Club at Totternhoe near Dunstable.

The Austin and South Birmingham Motor-Cycle Club held two events at the Austin playing fields on Lowhill Lane, Rednal. These meetings were staged on 28 April and 8 September, with the objective of the club being to provide motor-cycling sport at a price that the average amateur could afford to pay. Entrance to meetings was not just confined to the employees of the Austin Motor company either. The race meeting on 28 April included three famous riders in Syd Jackson (348cc AJS), Wal Morton (348cc AJS) and Billy Dallison (348cc Calthorpe), who all went on to become well-known speedway riders.

With reference to the Witney Concrete Speedway, this was a unique circuit which was partly grass and partly concrete, and a section of the track even went through an old barn at the old Witney Aerodrome.

Blackpool and Fylde Motor Club ran meetings on Saturdays at Blackpool Trotting Sports Ground, with the surface consisting of sand, rather than shale. The circuit measured half a mile in length and was oval-shaped, in a similar manner to speedway tracks.

The Bath and West Club ran three meetings at Lansdown, on the outskirts of the city. The North Derbyshire Motor-Cycle Club staged their first meeting on 14 July at Wingerworth, near Chesterfield, prior to holding a second event on 8 August. Racing was also staged for the first time at Harraby Stadium in Carlisle on 21 July.

Harrogate & District Motor Cycle Club.

(Affiliated to the A.C.U. and Members of Yorks. Centre).

ENTRY FORM.
FOR
MOTOR CYCLE RACES
TO BE HELD ON

The Cricket Field, St. George's Road, off Leeds Road,

By kind permission of the Harrogate Cricket and Athletic Club, on

Saturday, August 18th, 1928,

er the General Competition Rules of the Auto-Cycle Union, and Restricted Permit, No......

Racing Commences at 3 p.m. prompt.

COMPETITORS WILL BE GRADED.

Open to the following Clubs :

Leeds, Bradford, Huddersfield, York, Tadcaster and Harrogate.

Entries Close First Post Wednesday, August 15th, certain.

W. MILNER, Hon. Secretary,

17 West Cliffe Terrace,

Harrog

Harrogate programme, 1928.

TADCASTER DISTRICT MOTOR CLUB

Affiliated to the A.C.U. and Members of the Yorks. Centre A.C.U.

PRESIDENT : ARTHUR PROCTER, ESQ.

Will hold a Meeting for

MOTOR CYCLE
Grass Track Racing

Open to Members of Clubs affiliated to

THE YORKSHIRE CENTRE A.C.U.,

On Saturday, August 11th,

1928, at the

Ings Race Track, Tadcaster.

Upwards of £100 in Prizes.

GRAND PARADE of all Competitors at 3 p.m., prior to First Race.

ADMISSION TO GROUND, ONE SHILLING.

Hon. Secretary :—H. D. HILL, KIRKGATE, TADCASTER.

Head-quarters :—Falcon Hotel, Chapel Street, Tadcaster.

Tadcaster programme, 1928.

1928 Roll Of Honour

British Open Championships (Belle Vue)
250cc – L. Higgs
350cc – Syd Jackson
500cc – Oliver Langton
Unlimited – F. Sissons
Sidecar – Wilf Mcclure
Sidecar Unlimited – I. Williamson

Tadcaster Championship Belt
Oliver Langton

Witney Concrete Speedway Championship
H. French

Oxted, Westerham & Limpsfield Carnall Trophy
R. Waters

Northern Championship
Alec Jackson

3
GRASS-TRACK RACING
1929

There was plenty of action all over Britain and the highlights included the Dunstable Club's August meeting, when Crystal Palace speedway aces Roger Frogley and Les Bowden took on the local champion, G.H. Grace. However, it was the local man, Grace, who dominated the event, winning the 350cc Class, Unlimited Class, Championship final and 350cc Handicap final.

A crowd of over 1,500 spectators watched racing at Wymering Park, organized by the Portsmouth Club. K. Purser won both the 350cc and 600cc finals on a Velocette. In Wiltshire, the North Wilts Motor-Cycle and Light Car Club held a meeting in aid of the local hospital, at the former Bath and West Agricultural Showground in Swindon. Denis Winslow emerged from that particular meeting as the top rider.

Ashford in Kent was a popular grass-track venue, with the Kent Motor Club holding a fair few meetings during the year. The local top rider was A.S. Bacon, who raced on an Ariel. A rider who would go on and race up until the late 1970s was George Wilks. He was doing well in 1929, winning a Grand Prix in front of 2,000 fans at Hammond's Farm, Sandridge in St Albans. In the southwest, Cyril England, mounted on an AJS, won the Croft Silver Medal at Yeovil.

Grass-track racing had well and truly arrived and there simply isn't enough room to list all the clubs that were holding race meetings. However, some of the more notable ones include Uxbridge (Hillingdon), Margate (Ash), North Bucks (Bletchley), Penistone Moorland (Yorkshire), Grimsby and Cleethorpes (Humberstone), Lancaster and Morecambe, Barnet (North London), Doncaster, Derby, Camberley, Redditch (Worcestershire) and Blackmore Vale (Shaftesbury).

The Blackmore Vale meetings were held at the Show Field in Shaftesbury, before the ever-popular Cannfield circuit was used. Tom Bryant was a winner at Blackmore, taking both the Sidecar and Unlimited solo finals, using O.K. Supreme machines. Two other names that featured in the history of the Blackmore Vale Club were P. Farquharson (Scott), who won the Novice final ahead of Nelson Cruse (BSA).

A club which has been a credit to the sport, right up to the present day, is the Evesham Motor-Cycle and Light Car Club in south Worcestershire. In 1929, they organized a meeting at Pershore Racecourse, which was watched by an estimated 3,000 people.

Finally, the North Derbyshire Club ran grass-track events on 7 July and 17 August at Wilmot's Farm, Grassmore, with the venue subsequently becoming known as Grassmore Speedway.

TADCASTER DISTRICT MOTOR CLUB.

(Affiliated to the A.C.U. and Members of the
Yorkshire Centre A.C.U.)

Official Programme 3d.

YORKSHIRE CENTRE
**Motor Cycle
Grass Track Races**

Open to Clubs in Membership of the Yorkshire
Centre A.C.U. (PERMIT No. R.A. 13),
SATURDAY, AUGUST 17th, 1929,
COMMENCING AT 3 P.M.

OFFICIALS.

PRESIDENT: ARTHUR PROCTER.
PRESIDENT YORKSHIRE CENTRE A.C.U.: FRANK WRIGHT
(York).

STEWARDS:
Appointed by the Yorkshire Centre A.C.U.—
F. W. RYAN (Middlesbrough), President-Elect Yorkshire Centre A.C.U.

Appointed by the Tadcaster D.M.C.—
H. W. ROBINSON (Ilkley), Past President Yorkshire Centre A.C.U.
FRED CLEVELAND (York), H. KIDSON (V.P. Tadcaster).

JUDGES:
H. PAYNE (Otley), V.P. Yorkshire Centre; H. BOWMAN, V.P. Tadcaster
D.M.C.; J. SHEARSMITH, V.P. Tadcaster and York.

STARTER:
C. B. WATSON (Tadcaster). Starter's Clerk: H. WRIGHT.
Time-keeper: B. W. O. RIDER.
I/c Colours: W. W. IREDALE.
Hon. Medical Officer: Dr. PHILLIPS
(V.P. Tadcaster D.M.C.), assisted by the Members of the Tadcaster V.A.D

Marshals:
A. SHACKLETON (VP. Tadcaster D.M.C.), G. HILL, W. WALKER,
C. GRIMSTON, C. STUTTARD, P. ALLEN, N. MUSTO,
T. H. BATTYE, G. H. BATTYE, G. WOOLFORD, G. TOES,
J. MENZIES, and Members of Yorkshire Centre Clubs.

Hon. Treasurer: J. H. LISTER, Wetherby Road, Tadcaster.
Assistant Hon. Secretary: A. HOWARD.
Hon. Secretary and Clerk of the Course—
H. D. HILL, Kirkgate, Tadcaster.

Tadcaster programme, 1929.

1929 Roll Of Honour

Camberley Victoria Cup
R. Holme

Croft Silver Medal (Yeovil)
Cyril England

Redditch Grand Prix
V.C. Morris

Three Pears Cup (Evesham MCC)
A.R. Taylor

Evesholme Cup (Evesham MCC)
Charlie Bower

Margate Motor Club Ash Solo Championship
C. Philpot

Kent Motor Club June Grand Championship
A.S. Bacon

Nomad Motor Club Grand Prix
C.K.I. Hawes

Bindford Motor Club Grand Prix
Eddie Flintoff

Austin Longbridge Silver Cup
L. Hadley

Lantillar Motor Club Grand Prix and Championship
A. Barker

Streatham Grand Prix
E. Langman

Southgate Grand Prix
C. Martin

Wood Green Grand Prix
P. Cornell

Blackmore Vale Club Championship
A.C. Titt

Dunstable Championship
G.H. Grace

Margate Solo Championship Silver Cup
J. Hanson

Austin & South Birmingham MCC Englebach Cup
W.H. Leadbitter

Austin & South Birmingham MCC Lickey Silver Cup
E. Mountford

4
GRASS-TRACK RACING
1930

The season started with the York Club's meeting at Atcombe on Good Friday, when the competitors included Tommy Gamble, M.E. Crossland and Sam Marsland. Although it was a cold day, some 3,000 spectators braved the chill to enjoy some good racing. That attendance was bettered, however, on a wet Easter Monday, when the North Wilts Club held a meeting at the Polo ground in Swindon, when an estimated crowd of 5,000 viewed the action. Ivor Webb, who was based near Cirencester, was victorious in both the 500cc Class and Unlimited Novice finals.

In the Southern Centre, the local mayor and mayoress presented the trophies at the Blackmore Vale grass-track, where a future star appeared in the novice final and finished second. Mounted on a Rayleigh, his name was Mike Erskine.

Up in Yorkshire, a rider by the name of Alec Hill from Harrogate, was winning the local awards, including the Golden Helmet and the Scott Trophy. In the Bexley Heath Club's event at Crayford Grass Speedway, H.L. Daniel (Norton) of road racing fame, won both the Chelsea and Westminster Cup races.

One of the most famous speedway venues started to host grass-track meetings in 1930 – Rocky Park at St Austell in Cornwall. In the programme from 16 August, event number six saw a Mr Williams of St Blazey, riding a 550cc Ariel, challenge all-comers over a two-mile course. The top point-scorer from this meeting was presented with a Silver Cup donated by N.G. Youlden. Racing continued to be held at the picturesque venue throughout the 1930s and after the war, right up until the end of 1948.

Remaining in Cornwall, the Pendennis Motor-Cycle and Light Car Club ran their first event on Thursday 7 August. The meeting was staged at the Recreation Ground in Falmouth and saw Bill Wilmott win both his heat and the final of the Unlimited Class, before also taking victory in the Handicap final.

The Bishop's Waltham Club was formed in October and seventeen-year-old Pat Holloway won the club's first-ever event. At the age of eighteen, another rider was just beginning his long career in 1930, as Bill Evans began solo racing. Mounted on a 1928 Rudge, Evans took second place in the 500cc Class of the Moseley and District Motor-Cycle Club's autumn meeting. Evans would, of course, go on to become a future sidecar champion of the 1950s.

Meetings were held at a variety of places all around Britain in 1930, including Loughborough, Maidstone, Sittingbourne, Plymouth, Widnes, Bournemouth, Barnet, Bristol, St Albans, Longbridge (Birmingham), East Fife, Redhill, Bury, Alphington (Nr Exeter), Tickenham (Bristol), Whitehaven and Northampton.

Harrogate Motor Cycle and Car Club

(Affiliated to the A.C.U. and Member of the Y.C. A.C.U.)

Grass Track Races

WEDNESDAY, AUG. 20th, 1930.

Harrogate programme, 1930.

1930 Roll Of Honour

South Midlands Championship (Barnet)
250cc – H. Knight
350cc – George Wilks
Club – Watford

Bournemouth Championship
350cc – R. Avery
600cc – L.C. Lovell

Southern Centre Championship
Solo – Wally Waring
Team – Ringwood

York Motor Club Golden Gauntlet
Sam Marsland

Plymouth Motor Club Mayors Handicap Cup
J.H. Kneebone

John Bull Challenge Trophy (Bath & Avon MCC)
Bill Hamblin

Frank Hallam Challenge Cup (Austin & South Birmingham MCC)
W. Tidesley

Camberley Blue Riband Challenge
Eddy Lawrence

Moorland Speed Trophy
G.B. Mortimer

North-East London MCC Grand Prix
Expert – George Wilks
Amateur – L.J. Johnson

East Fife Motor Club Championships
250cc – J.W. Stuart
350cc – Jo Nicol
600cc – J.W. Stuart

Brighton Unlimited Cup
D.J. Watson

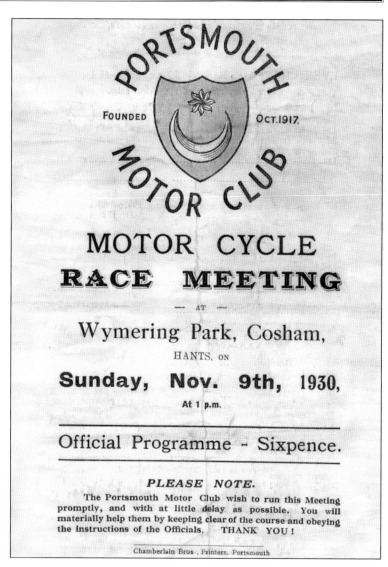

Wymering Park programme, 1930.

PORTSMOUTH
MOTOR CLUB

FOUNDED   OCT.1917.

MOTOR CYCLE
RACE MEETING

— AT —

Wymering Park, Cosham,

HANTS, ON

Sunday, Nov. 9th, 1930,

At 1 p.m.

Official Programme - Sixpence.

PLEASE NOTE.

The Portsmouth Motor Club wish to run this Meeting promptly, and with at little delay as possible. You will materially help them by keeping clear of the course and obeying the instructions of the Officials. THANK YOU!

Chamberlain Bros., Printers, Portsmouth

SCARBOROUGH and District MOTOR CLUB.

President: J. PICKERING.

(Affiliated to the Auto-Cycle Union, and Members of the Yorkshire Centre, A.C.U.).

With the support of the SCARBOROUGH CORPORATION, the above Club will hold

GRASS TRACK RACES

For Solo Motor Cycles,

On Tuesday, August 5th, 1930.

at 3 p.m.

on the Corporation Sports Ground, Burniston Road, Scarborough, (near Peasholm Park).

Open to Members of the following Seven Clubs :—
Bradford & District ; Hull Auto-Cycle ; Leeds ;
Pickering ; Scarborough ; Tadcaster ; York.
Yorkshire Centre Restricted Permit No. R.294.

The Event will be held under the General Competition Rules of the Auto-Cycle Union and the Supplementary Regulations herewith.

Headquarters for the Event :—The "Salisbury" Hotel, Huntriss Row, Scarborough.
Organiser and Secretary for the Meeting (to whom all Entries and Enquiries must be sent) :—
W. A. DOVENER, Avenue House, Woodhouse Lane, Leeds.
(Phone: Leeds 23134).

Entries positively close First Post Friday, August 1st.

Scarborough advert, 1930.

George Buck leading Charlie Bower at Rushmere.

Arthur Goddard leads Charlie Bower at Rushmere.

YORKSHIRE CENTRE
A.C.U.

President: W. RYAN (Middlesbrough).

YORK MOTOR CLUB.
Affiliated to the A.C.U.
Members of the Yorkshire Centre.

President: FRANK WRIGHT

YORKSHIRE CENTRE

GRASS TRACK RACES

ORGANISED BY THE YORK MOTOR CLUB.

IN AID OF THE YORK COUNTY HOSPITAL.

Open to Members of Clubs in the Yorkshire Centre.

(Under Auto Cycle Union General Competition Rules).

Near ACOMB, York,

3 Miles West of York, on the Main Wetherby Road,

On SUNDAY, AUGUST 24th, 1930,

Commencing **3** o'clock prompt.

Grand Parade of all Competitors prior to First Race.

Admission to Course, One Shilling.   Children Sixpence.

Hon. Secretary:
S. FROST, 7, BRIDGE STREET, YORK. (Tel. 2203).

Headquarters: Black Swan Hotel, Coney Street, York.   (Tel. 2220).

ENTRIES CLOSE TUESDAY, AUGUST 19th, 1930.

York advert, 1930.

5
GRASS-TRACK RACING
1931

One of the oldest A.C.U. Centre Championships, the South Midlands, was in full swing with this year's event, run at the Barnet Grass Speedway. George Wilks became the 250cc champion, but in the 350cc Class, he fell while leading and handed the title to J.H. Balmer (Rudge). The up-to-600cc Championship went to C. Traynor (Rudge) and, although he didn't win, the crowd really enjoyed the spectacular leg-trailing broadsides of speedway legend George Newton, who was also mounted on a Rudge machine.

At the Sarum Club's first meeting at Salisbury, Wiltshire on 18 July, Paddy Cash took the honours in no less than five categories, in front of 1,500 enthusiastic grass fans. On the mechanical side, non-skid devices used on the wheels were banned by the authorities.

On the English/Welsh border, the Severn Valley Motor-Cycle and Light Car Club organized a meeting at the Recreation Ground in Welshpool. The track was a third of a mile in length and very rough, but it didn't stop Bernard Corfield (Excelsior) from winning the 350cc and 500cc Classes, as well as the Welshpool Championship.

Down in the south-east, one of the most popular venues was the Sydenham Motor Club's mountain grass-track at Layham's Farm. Average speeds for the challenging circuit ranged between 40-50mph.

The Leiston & District Motor Club ran an Eastern Centre Inter-Club Championship, with riders representing Ipswich, Ilford, Norfolk and Leiston, among others. The winner of the 500cc Championship was D.W. Sampson of Ipswich, who rode a Norton machine. Runner-up was A.L. Milk (Velo), while Roy Baker (Sunbeam) was third.

Another famous venue, situated in the north, was the Squires Gate Aerodrome, where meetings were conducted by the Blackpool Motor-Cycle and Light Car Club. In 1931, they ran at least five meetings, when a regular competitor was speedway legend Bill Kitchen.

Carnival grass-tracks were always popular, right up until the 1970s. In 1931, the Bournemouth Club held an event in conjunction with the Boscombe Carnival at King's Park Sports Ground. Cecil Barrow (Royal Enfield) was the victor in both the 350cc and 500cc finals. Nearby, at Poulner, the Ringwood Club held a meeting at the annual flower show, with Barrow again cleaning up in the 350cc and 500cc Classes. The Ringwood Club, incidentally, later won the Southern Centre Championship Team Shield.

Talking of carnivals, down in Cornwall, the Pendennis Club organized racing at the Recreation Ground, Falmouth, as part of Falmouth Carnival week, which took place in August.

By 1931, the Evesham Club were running their events at Crown Meadow, having moved from their previous venue at Pershore Racecourse.

A rider who embarked on a career that would later see him crowned as a sidecar champion was Eric Oliver, who started in the solo classes.

YORK MOTOR CLUB.

President   FRANK WRIGHT, Esq.

Affiliated to the A.C.U.   Members of the Yorkshire Centre A.C.U.

Headquarters:

BLACK SWAN HOTEL, CONEY STREET, YORK (Tel. 2220).

FOUNDED 1913.

SEASON 1931.

AUGUST PROGRAMME.

Monday, August 3rd (Bank Holiday). Grass Track Races organised by the Scarborough Motor Club, on the Corporation Sports Ground, Burniston Road. Open to Members of our Club. First Race 3 p.m.

Tuesday, August 18th, Committee Meeting at 7-30.

Sunday, August 23rd. Yorkshire Centre Event at "Post Hill," organised by the Leeds Motor Club. First Race 3 p.m.

Wednesday, August 26th, MOTOR CYCLE GYMKHANA, on the Club's Racing Track at Wetherby Road, commence at 6-45 p.m. Entries taken on the Field for Potato Races, Obstacle Races, Musical Chairs, etc. Cash Prizes will be given. Bring your friends to see the fun.

Sunday, August 30th. Social Outing to Fraisthorpe Sands, near Bridlington. Bring food and bathing costumes. Meet at St. Sampson's Square at 10 a.m.
The 55 Members and Friends who went on this outing in June will remember the glorious day we had.

During July we had three Social Outings. The first an Evening Trip to Birdsall Hall, the second to Kirkham Abbey, where thanks to Mr and Mrs Sydney Clay, we had the use of their Motor Launch and had a most enjoyable day, and the third to Rosedale Abbey to meet the Middlesbrough Club and have an impromptu Hill Climb on Rosedale Chimney.

Although the weather has not been too kind this season, we have had a fair muster on our Social Outings, but hope that for the remaining ones, that even larger numbers will turn out. We make an effort to make these trips entertaining, so come along and join the happy band.

NOTE —We are holding Grass Track Races on Sunday, September 13th, keep this date open. Pin this Programme up, so that you will always have the events for the month before you.

Telephone 2203.
7, BRIDGE STREET,
YORK.

FOR THE YORK MOTOR CLUB,
STANLEY FROST,
Hon. Secretary.

York advert, 1931.

1931 Roll Of Honour

South Midlands Championships (Barnet)
250cc – George Wilks
350cc – J.H. Balmer
600cc – C. Traynor
Club – Watford

Southern Centre Championship
Team Shield – Ringwood

Lancaster & Morecambe Golden Helmet
Bill Kitchen

Boscombe Carnival
350cc – Cecil Barrow
500cc – Cecil Barrow

Garstang Agricultural Show
350cc – Bill Kitchen
500cc – J. Quarmby

Scarborough Grand Prix
George Reynard

Waterlooville Wymering Grand Prix
Wally Waring

North Berks Motor Club Grand Prix
J.H. White

Camberley Silver Helmet
W. Neale

Bradford Grand Prix
Alan Jefferies

Welshpool Championship
Bernard Corfield

PROGRAMME

CARSHALTON MOTOR CYCLE CLUB

The Fifth Grass Track Meeting

at CARSHALTON'S ADDINGTON TRACK

(Top of Lodge Lane, opposite Addington Church.)

On SUNDAY, SEPTEMBER 20th, 1931

First Race 3 p.m.

Open to members of the
SOUTH EASTERN CENTRE A.C.U.

South Eastern Centre (A.C.U.) . . Permit No. 661
Held under the General Competition Rules of the A.C.U.

OFFICIALS :

Judges : A. Sharman, G. M. Cook.
Club Stewards : **W. V. Pickering, W. F. Guiver.**
S.E. Centre Steward : **H. N. Edwards.**
Paddock Marshal : **W. F. Plumb.**   Starter : **C. B. Freeman.**
Machine Examiner : **A. D. Weston.**   Chief Marshal : **F. W. Dyer.**
Timekeeper : **F. L. Dodridge.**   Clerk of the Course : **H. J. Green.**
Treasurer : **C. W. Petzold.**
Secretary of the Meeting : **H. E. R. Polden,** 84 Beverstone Road, Thornton Heath.

The Carshalton M.C.C. desires to thank competitors,
officials, and the St. John's Ambulance Brigade for
their co-operation and assistance at this meeting.

SPECTATORS   Admission 1/3 (INCLUDING PROGRAMME and Tax)   **Parking Free.**

Spectators are not allowed to drive about the field. Mind the bumps !   Parking round the track within 10ft. of the ropes

---

CATERING by Messrs C. F. NORWOOD at Popular Prices.
Tents for the convenience of Ladies and Gentlemen have been erected, near the track.

Addington programme, 1931.

6
GRASS-TRACK RACING
1932

This year witnessed the first-ever Worcestershire Championship, organized by the Evesham Club. Bob Foster won the event, although, for some strange reason, the name on the trophy says F. Pratt!

Another major launch this year was the Brands Hatch Combine, which was made up of the West Kent, Sidcup, Owls and Bermondsey clubs. Their first meeting took place on Easter Monday, when the winners were R.L. Briggs (250cc and 350cc), V.A. Bryant (600cc and Grand Prix) and R. Young (Sidecar).

Some tracks have gone down in history as the ones that folk always talk about, and one of these was Cannards Grave in Shepton Mallet. Riders that did well at this popular Wessex venue included R.J. Stone, Cyril England, Rex King and Trowbridge-based G.J. Sleightholme.

Although Rocky Park was the famous venue in Cornwall at this time, the Mid-Cornwall Motor-Cycle and Light Car Club also organized meetings at Newquay.

Racing was again popular, especially in the southeast of England at Brands Hatch and Layham's Farm, but most A.C.U. centres were organizing events throughout Britain – not just in England, but also in Wales and Scotland. In Wales, larger clubs at Swansea, Newport and Cardiff organized meetings, but some of the smaller clubs also ran events. These included Ogmore and District Motor-Cycle Club and Gwendraeth Valley Motor-Cycle and Light Car Club, who were stationed in Llanelli.

1932 also saw the opening of the Cannfield circuit, with meetings being promoted by the Blackmore Vale Club.

One of the major events of the year was the Yorkshire Championship. The meeting was affected by rain, but it didn't stop Bill Kitchen, mounted on a Rudge, from lifting the *Yorkshire Evening Post* Trophy, after he had defeated J. Quarmby and Alec Hill. Initially, Tommy Gamble had led the race on his Jap machine, but an engine failure let Kitchen through to take the spoils of victory.

Down in the south, Cecil Barrow was again a victor in the Boscombe Carnival, although he was a trifle fortunate when another local ace, Leslie Jones, suffered from mechanical gremlins. Staying in the south, the West of England Motor Club event at Kingsteignton saw a future speedway star show his paces, when Broncho Slade (Humber) took second place in the 350cc Class. Slade later went on to win the Consolation final at Tedburn St Mary, near Exeter, this time mounted on a Rudge.

Team racing was starting to get popular and one such event took place at Southampton, when the homesters defeated Sarum (Salisbury) by 51 points to 37. The same meeting also saw Cirencester rider Ivor Webb emerge triumphant from the 350cc final.

GRASS

TRACK

RACE

MEETING

HELD AT

"The Downlands,"

:: Snell's Corner, ::

Horndean,   Hants,

ON

Sunday, September 4th, 1932.

FIRST RACE 2.30 P.M.

Circuit approximately ¼ mile   All races 4 laps run anti-clockwise

OFFICIAL   PROGRAMME : : : SIXPENCE.

Spectators are earnestly requested to keep outside the ropes, otherwise the organisers
cannot accept liability for their safety.

Horndean programme, 1932.

In August, Tommy Kessell and Alf Hugh used older machines when they scored 19 and 11 points respectively, as Cornwall defeated Devon in a team meeting at St Austell's Rocky Park. Kessell was mounted on a 1926 Zenith machine, while Hugh was on board a 1924 New Imperial.

On Thursday 1 September, Australian Bert Jones, who was living in Cornwall, raced on a dirt-track Rudge machine – this was, in fact, the very first time that a dirt-track (or speedway) bike had been used on the grass in that particular part of the country.

In the Wessex Centre, the Trowbridge Motor-Cycle Club organized a rare event at West Ashton Road. Entrants included Cyril England, Ivor Webb, Tom Bryant and Mike Erskine. Prize money for the event was £2 for match races and £1 for all other first places, plus a challenge cup for the fastest time of the day. The meeting also included an interval demonstration by eight-year-old Tink Bryant.

An interesting item appeared in the book *A History of Reading Speedway*, when historian Les Hawkins discovered that grass-track racing took place at Tilehust in Reading on 16 May 1932. This was at the very same stadium that was to be the home of Reading speedway some thirty-six years later, in 1968.

1932 Roll Of Honour

Worcestershire Championship
Bob Foster

Yorkshire Evening Post Championship
Bill Kitchen

Retford Club Champion
Fred Tate

Southern Centre Championships
Team Shield – Bishop's Waltham

Middlesbrough Motor Club Golden Sash
A. Hill

Keighley Grand Prix & All-Star Championship
B. Holden

Boscombe Carnival
500cc – Cecil Barrow
Open – Cecil Barrow

Irish 20 Mile Championship
J.D. Burney

Chester Championship
G. Smith

North-East Motor-Cycle Club Grand Prix
R.A. Scott

Gravesend Solo Championship
Wally Lock

Brownhills Silver Gauntlet
H. Huntley

Brownhills Golden Helmet
W. Murphy

Brands Hatch Opening Championships
250cc – R.L. Briggs
350cc – V.A. Bryant
600cc – V.A. Bryant
Grand Prix – V.A. Bryant
Sidecar – R. Young

SYDENHAM MOTOR CLUB.
(Affiliated to S.E. Centre A.C.U.)

Open~to~Centre

MOUNTAIN MILE GRAND PRIX MEETING
HELD AT
LAYHAM'S FARM, WEST WICKHAM, KENT,
on **SUNDAY, MAY 22nd, 1932.**

Start 2.0 p.m.   *Price 3d.*

The Journal with the Green Cover.

Published
EVERY WEDNESDAY - 3d.

Regular features of "Motor Cycling" include:—

News of the Week.
Sports Gossip by "Cyclops."
Reports of all Big Events.
Club Notes and News.
Current Topics by "Carbon."
Around the Speedways.
Information and Advice.

Offices of "MOTOR CYCLING."
5-15, ROSEBERY AVENUE, LONDON, E.C.1

Layham's Farm programme, 1932.

THE TROWBRIDGE MOTOR CYCLE CLUB.

GRASS TRACK RACES

SATURDAY, JUNE 25th, 1932,

West Ashton Road, Trowbridge

(FIELD KINDLY LOANED BY T. C. CORP, ESQ.)

OFFICIALS:-

Wessex Centre, A.C.U. Representative	C. H. KING, ESQ.
Judges - P. M. SNAILUM, ESQ. & H. WESTLAKE RICHARDS, ESQ.	
Clerk of the Course	A. LYE, ESQ.
Competitors' Stewards - R. COLES, ESQ., D. EASTON, ESQ., H. FRANCIS, ESQ.	
Timekeeper	LIEUT.-COL. W. H. MANN, M.C.
Starter	E. SELMAN, ESQ.
Secretaries of the Meeting	G. H. MILLINGTON, ESQ., AND
	G. SLEIGHTHOLME, ESQ.

——— **PROGRAMME 2d.** ———

T. R. DIPLOCK, PRINTER, TROWBRIDGE.

Trowbridge programme, 1932.

7
GRASS-TRACK RACING
1933

One of the first meetings of 1933 was organized by the Bishop's Waltham Motor Club, with Paddy Cash tasting victory in the Tom Duke Challenge Trophy match race, defeating Leslie Jones and C. Pearce. Team racing was also on the menu, with Bishop's Waltham beating a team known as The Rest, by 8 points to 7.

In the early years, it was the solos that stole the glory, but a certain Harold Taylor made a name for himself when winning the Silver Wings at the Layham's Farm Mountain Mile with his sidecar outfit. That was, in fact, the only time that a sidecar outfit ever achieved this feat. As far as the solos were concerned, Harold Daniell was making a habit of winning the Silver Wings in 1933.

Big crowds were reported all over the United Kingdom – in the north, there were 5,000 people at Darlington; in the south east, 3,000 fans turned up at Brands Hatch; while in the north west, racing at Blackpool attracted 2,000 specatators. In fact, the Blackpool Motor-Cycle and Light Car Club were still running their events at Squires Gate and another speedway ace, Joe Abbott, was successful in several of their finals.

In the 1960s the Worcester Auto Club ran meetings at Raven Meadow. However, in 1933, meetings were run at the very same venue, but by the Worcester Co-Op Motor-Cycle and Light Car Club. The top man from Worcester, both before and after the Second World War, was Reg Lambourne, who was later to appear for Swindon Speedway when they opened at Blunsdon in 1949.

During July, the Canterbury Motor Club organized a meeting that featured the Canterbury Championship. The event was won by S.H. Blacklocks, who overcame a strong challenge from Tom Arter (of road racing fame).

In south Wales, Eddie Thomas won the prestigious Swansea Championship, but a man who was starting to win a lot of finals was Norman Treseder Snr, who was mounted on a Douglas.

Clubs that staged racing this year included Sarum (High Post, at the old aerodrome), South Reading (California Sand-Track), Blackmore Vale (Cannfield), Harrogate, Pontefract, Dunstable, St Austell (Rocky Park), North Berks Amateur (Wantage), Cygnet (Rushmere), Hungerford, Sarum (Salisbury) and Ringwood.

The year's South-Eastern Centre Championships were held at the Sydenham Club's Layham's Farm circuit at West Wickham. S.H. Blacklocks took the Individual Championship on a 499cc Cotton, while Les Schwieso (346cc A.J.S.) was second, and Jock West (497cc Hartley Ariel) finished third. Class winners at the event were: 175cc – Ken Frogley (Francis Barnett); 250cc – Triss Sharp (Malvern Cotton); 350cc – Wally Lock (Velo); 500cc – Harold Taylor (Norton); Unlimited Sidecars – Harold Taylor (Norton).

The Sydenham Layham's Championship and Matchless Cup produced some

Portsmouth, Albatross and Waterlooville Motor Clubs.

RACE MEETING

AT

WYMERING PARK RACECOURSE

(By kind permission of G. Cooper, Esq.)

ON

Sunday, October 15th, 1933.

FIRST EVENT 2 p.m. PROMPT.

Organised under Southern Centre A.C.U. Permit R 473, and the Rules of the A.C.U., and Track Racing Rules of the Southern Centre A.C.U.

OFFICIALS OF THE MEETING.

A.C.U. Steward—E. N. L. Guymer, Esq.

Club Stewards—C. R. Jones; L. Burnett; G. Beech.

Timekeepers—W. West; R. Maunder, Senr.; F. Williams.

Pit Marshals—W. Waring and A. T. Bull.

Clerk of the Meeting—R. H. Dorey, 102 Madeira Road, North End, Portsmouth.

Machine Examiner—R. Burnett.

—o—

OFFICIAL PROGRAMME — TWOPENCE.

CHAMBERLAIN BROS., SOUTHSEA.

Wymering Park programme, 1933.

THE WEST WILTS MOTOR CLUB.

GRASS TRACK RACES

SATURDAY, JUNE 24th, 1933,

West Ashton Road, Trowbridge

(FIELD KINDLY LOANED BY T. C. CORP, ESQ.)

OFFICIALS:-

President	MRS. S. W. APPLEGATE.
Wessex Centre, A.C.U. Representative	S. JENKINS, Esq.
Judges	P. M. SNAILUM, Esq., and MRS. SNAILUM.
Competitors' Stewards	R. COLES, Esq., J. AYRES, Esq., R. OWEN. Esq.
Timekeeper and Handicapper	V. C. ANSTICE, Esq.
Starter	W. J. WILLIAMS, Esq.
Secretary of Meeting	G. H. MILLINGTON. Esq.
Radio Amplifier	BY MESSRS. JAMES BROS., (WILTSHIRE) LTD.

PROGRAMME 2d.

T. R. DIPLOCK, PRINTER, TROWBRIDGE.

Trowbridge programme, 1933.

interesting results, with Triss Sharp tasting victory in the Lightweight Class, while Bill Merrett won the Junior event. The Senior Matchless event was won by George Rayner, with the Sidecar event being won by Les Chapman.

In Cornwall at Rocky Park, team events were becoming extremely popular with the spectators, and matches included St Austell *v.* Ringwood, and Cornwall *v.* Devon. Cornish champions of the year were Bob Collins, Bert Jones and Tommy Kessell.

The Blackmore Vale Motor-Cycle Club staged a team event against Sarum, and in a very close encounter it was the homesters who won by 41 points to 39. Staying with Blackmore Vale, Paddy Cash lifted the prestigious Peto Trophy in 1933.

At the Brands Hatch Championships, Wally Lock took victory in both the 350cc and 500cc categories, while S.H. Goddard was triumphant in the 250cc Class.

1933 Roll Of Honour

Worcestershire Championship
Bob Foster

Cornish Championships
Morcum Shield & Cornwall County Challenge – Bob Collins
W. Vivian Unlimited Cup & Phillips 500cc Cup – Bert Jones
County Garage 350cc Cup – Tommy Kessell

Moseley & District Championships
Club Championship - W. Webb
Grand Prix – H.J. Robinson

Swansea Championship
Eddie Thomas

Darlington Championships
Grand Prix – J.Reynolds
Willow Bridge Handicap – Bill Kitchen

Hungerford Carnival
R. Rosier

Canterbury Championship
S.H. Blacklocks

Newcastle-Upon-Tyne North Mail Championship
R. Craig

Bishop's Waltham Championships
Challenge Cup & Tom Duke Challenge Cup – Paddy Cash
Challenge Trophy – Mike Erskine

South-Eastern Centre Championships
175cc – Ken Frogley
250cc – Triss Sharp
350cc – Wally Lock
Individual – S.H. Blacklocks
500cc & Unlimited Sidecar – Harold Taylor
Club – Sidcup

Camberley Grand Prix
J.G. Smith

Honiton Silver Cup
Reg Robins

South Midlands Centre Championships
250cc – George Wilks
350cc – R.A. Scott
600cc – C. Traynor
Club – West Herts

Southern Centre Championships
Individual – Paddy Cash
Team Shield – Waterlooville

PORTSMOUTH MOTOR CLUB.

GRASS TRACK

RACE MEETING

HELD AT THE

Greyhound and Sports' Stadium

TARGET ROAD, STAMSHAW,

ON

Sunday, December 10th, 1933.

FIRST EVENT 2 p.m. PROMPT.

Organised under Permit No. R   of the Southern Centre A.C.U. and subject to all rules and regulations of the A.C.U. and the Southern Centre Grass Track Racing Rules.

OFFICIALS OF THE MEETING.

A.C.U. Steward—
A. C. Abbott, Esq.

Club Steward—
A. D. Goyns, Esq.

Clerk of the Meeting—
R. H. Dorey,
102 Madeira Road, North End,
Portsmouth.

Starter—
C. R. Jones.

Timekeepers—
Messrs. W. West and R. Audas.

Handicapper—
D. West.

Pit Marshals—
Messrs. Norris and Burnett.

Machine Examiner—
R. Burnett.

Refreshments may be obtained at the Buffet during the course of this Meeting at popular prices.

—o—

OFFICIAL PROGRAMME — TWOPENCE.

Stamshaw programme, 1933.

Tommy Kessell.

Bob Collins.

8
GRASS-TRACK RACING
1934

This year saw the St Austell team of Bill Willmott, Bert Jones, A.W. Jones and S. Martin travel up to the Southern Centre and defeat a Ringwood side, 21-15. Sarum & District Motor-Cycle and Light Car Club changed its name to Salisbury Motor Club.

In south Wales, Eddie Thomas defeated Chris Boss and Roy Zeal at the Bridgend Hospital Carnival meeting, held on the local rugby field. Staying in Wales, a meeting was organized by the Carmarthen Motor-Cycle and Light Car Club at the famous Carmarthen Park, where the winners were D.W. Davies, Tom Lougher and Pip Lee.

The Barry Motor-Cycle Club also took part in team racing, travelling down to Rocky Park; however, the team led by Roy Zeal were soundly beaten (28-3) by St Austell. The victorious Cornish team consisted of Tommy Kessell, Wooshy Hugh, Bert Jones and Bob Collins. Appearing in the novice events was Ivan Kessell, who went on to have a successful speedway career with Plymouth.

In the south east, spectators were still flocking to Brands Hatch, where attendances ranged between 3,000 and 5,000 to watch the stars, such as Jock West, Wally Lock and Les Schweiso – the latter winning two Brands Hatch Championships during the year.

Up in the north west, successful meetings were held at Blackpool (Squires Gate) and Bury, while on the Wales/Cheshire border, racing was becoming popular at both Park Hall (Oswestry) and at Wrexham.

Emerging during the year was future speedway star and promoter Pete Lansdale, who started to win several grass finals in the eastern and south midland areas. The Evesham Club organized the Worcestershire Championship at Crown Meadow, with Bob Foster collecting another victory.

The Wessex Centre saw the Knowle & District Club organize meetings at Downend and Southmead, while the Fishponds & District Club held events at Drake's Farm, Westerleigh. A full programme of racing was again held at the Cannfield Speedway, as it was called, organized by the Blackmore Vale Club, situated near Shaftesbury in Dorset. Looking at the programme from 17 June (which cost 3d), the prize money varied from £2 to £5 for a win, the latter being more than a week's wages for some people in 1934. Paddy Cash, riding under the Club Albatross banner, won two of the finals at this meeting. Other well-known names in the meeting included the Sleightholme brothers, Jack Difazio, Leslie Jones, Pat Holloway, Ivor Webb and R.C. Dibben. The sidecar competitors included Oxfordshire's Johnny Browne. Sadly, Paddy Cash lost his life in an aeroplane crash shortly after this event.

Top riders Bill Kitchen and Mike Erskine made their first visits to Rocky Park in St Austell, where Bill Kitchen dominated his races. Included in Kitchen's triumphs were two match-race victories against Bill Willmott and Bert Jones.

Action from Graham's Farms, Stratford-upon-Avon, 1934.

The Shepton Mallet Motor-Cycle Club were again organizing meetings at Cannards Grave. On 11 July, Ivor Webb, mounted on his AJS, won all his heats and finals against top west country aces Difazio, Sleightholme and England. Prize money was £1 for a final win, while the open category had a first prize of £2.

In conjunction with Cardiff City Football Club, racing was held at Ninian Park, where Eddie Thomas, Roy Zeal and Pip Lee emerged as the top riders. One of the early pre-war meetings in the Western Centre was held at Cheltenham in June, while regular events were held at Worcester.

The Eastern Centre had a full programme of racing in 1934, with events at Southend, Hadleigh and Ilford. We must not forget the East Midlands Centre, which staged meetings at Grantham.

In another team event, the South Midlands defeated the South-East 37-14, in a meeting staged at Barnet Speedway. Another successful season in the south, saw the Southern Centre Championships held at the aptly named 'As you like it' Sports Club Ground, situated on the Ringwood to Fordingbridge Road. The Ringwood Club organized meetings locally at Linwood Farm, plus a joint venture at The Mount in Poulner, when they teamed up with the Blackmore Vale Motor-Cycle Club.

1934 Roll Of Honour

South-Eastern Championship
Wally Lock

Worcestershire Championship
Bob Foster

Cardiff Championships (Ninian Park)
Alex Thom Senior Trophy – Roy Zeal
350cc Junior Trophy – Eddie Thomas

Bishop's Waltham Championships
Tom Duke Challenge Cup – Paddy Cash

Bury Club Championship
Harold Jackson

Bridgend Hospital Carnival
350cc and 500cc – Eddie Thomas

Cornish Championships
Phillips 500cc, W. Vivian and Huddy & Kneebone Cups – Bert Jones
Morcum Shield – Bill Willmott
County Garage 350cc Cup – Tommy Kessell
Eustace Novice Cup – Ivan Kessell

Brands Hatch Championships
250cc – Alf Castle
350cc and 650cc – Les Schweiso
Sidecar – Arthur Horton
Club – Bermondsey

Northampton Pirates Championship
Bob Foster

Moseley Championships
Club Championship – A.J.Semot
Grand Prix – A.J. Wright

Yorkshire Centre Championship
Tommy Gamble

Barnet Grass Speedway Championship
Tommy Price

Southern Centre Team Shield
Waterlooville

RINGWOOD M.C. & L.C.C.

GRASS TRACK RACES

(Open to Southern Centre, A.C.U.)

LEAGUE EVENT.

AT

Linwood Farm, near Ringwood

(about three miles from Ringwood, route
dyed from " White Hart," Poulner)

— ON —

APRIL 29th, 1934

Varied Programme, including Sidecar/Threewheeler Race.

REFRESHMENTS and TEAS.   FIRST RACE 2-30 p.m.

FREE PARKING for all Vehicles.

Cars to the Ringside.

Admission, 1/3 ; Children, 6d.
(Including Tax).

CHACEWATER CHARLIE, the Comedy Cyclist, will perform.

Particulars from T. E. Mitchell, 23, Holdenhurst Road, Bournemouth.

Albany Press, Ringwood.

Ringwood advert, 1934.

9
GRASS-TRACK RACING
1935

In these pre-British Championship days, the Brands Hatch Championship was one of the major titles competed for, and over 4,000 people witnessed the 1935 event. The winner of the Individual Championship was Jock West (Ariel), while in the Sidecars event, Brian Ducker (Norton) defeated Jack Surtees (Jap) and George Taylor (Ariel).

Jock West was, indeed, the man to beat this year, as he also won the South-Eastern Centre Individual title the following month, in front of an even larger Brands Hatch crowd.

Earlier in the season on 5 May, the Sydenham Motor Club held their Grand Jubilee meeting at the Flying Mile circuit at Biggin Hill in Kent. There were several major trophies raced for: the Hampton Court Cup (200cc); Windsor Cup (250cc); Sandringham Cup (350cc); Jubilee Cup (Unlimited); Queen's Cup (Visitors Handicap); Balmoral Cup (Sidecars); Buckingham Cup (Second Sidecars); and King's Cup (Sidecar Handicap). A.H. Horton (Norton) won two of the Sidecar cups, while Les Schwieso won both the Jubilee and Sandringham Cups, averaging over 50mph. Looking at the programme, it was a terrific line-up at Biggin Hill and included Brian Ducker, Jack Surtees and W.J. Nethercott in the sidecars, with the solo racers including Tom Arter, S.H. Goddard and E.J. Cashman, who were all big stars in their day. Len Cole also took part in the event, on one of his faithful old Douglas machines.

In the Southern Centre Championships at Cannfield Speedway, Tommy Bounds (Norton) was triumphant in the Sidecar event, winning from Stan Bell (Excelsior). A future star of the Southern Centre also made his mark, when Bingley Cree took both the 350cc and Unlimited Expert Barred titles, mounted on Velocette machinery.

Down at Rocky Park in St Austell, top speedway riders taking on the locals became normal fare for the spectators, with visitors including George Wilks, Wal Phillips, Bill Kitchen and Percy Brine.

In the Midlands, the Evesham Club was now running events at Broadway Hill and pulling in some big crowds. Tommy Deadman was particularly successful in the June event at the new venue. Just down the road, the Worcester Club was still holding meetings at Raven Meadow and also at Rose Place Meadow, on the Droitwich Road. Slightly to the north, the King's Norton Club defeated a team called The Rest at Wythall.

Over at Hereford, the Wye Valley Auto Club had started organizing successful grass-track meetings. The Hereford Grand Prix on 25 June saw Tom Loughor taste victory on a Jap, with Colin Mead second on a 350cc AJS, while the Rudge-mounted Richie Reynolds finished third.

Moving north, J.H. Reynolds won the Yorkshire Championship, defeating W. Newby and Tommy Gamble at Scarborough. At the Coventry & Warwickshire's Maxstoke Castle

Another Magnificent Smashing Performance

BY

BILL KITCHEN

WHO IS RIDING AT

ST. AUSTELL SPEEDWAY

THIS THURSDAY, JULY 11th,

AT 6.15 P.M.

Five days after helping to win the Tests for England.

By marvellous riding last Saturday night he scored 10 points for England defeating Vix Huxley (The Australian Capt.) 3 times, (Huxley is recognised as being the greatest Speedway Rider the world has ever known,) and he had two wins over Tom Farndon (British Individual Champion,) and two over Max Grosskreutz.

In International and League Matches this season he has met and defeated every famous Speedway Star in Great Britain!!!

In the three International Speedway Tests, England v. Australia that have been held this season, he has been the **most consistent scorer in the Tests**. He has **scored more points for England** than any other rider having won Six 1sts, Six 2nds and Four 3rds, and has beaten the following International Stars : Vic Huxley (Australian Capt.) Seven times, Tom Farndon (British Individual Champion) Four times ; Lionel Van Praag, Four times ; Max Grosskreutz, Ron Johnson, Bluey Wilkinson, Jack Ormston, Three times each ; and Dicky Case, Jack Sharp, Frank Charles, Twice each.

SPECIAL—Flying Start Four Lap Match Race, BILL KITCHEN v. BERT JONES and an **EXHIBITION SOLO SPEED BURST** Flying Start by BILL KITCHEN.

Don't miss this wonderful opportunity of seeing the World's Greatest Motor Cycle Star at the very top of his form. You will never get another chance of seeing an International in action five days after he has ridden for England.

If you have never seen a Speedway before make a special effort to see the Greatest Grass Speedway Meeting ever organised in England.—You'll never forget it.

Admission 9d. inc. Tax., Cars 6d., Motor Cycles 3d., Children under 14, 2d.

W. & T. Sanders, Printers, St. Austell.

St Austell advert, 1935.

1935 shop window display in St Austell.

circuit in Coleshill, it was Freddie Hudson on his O.K. Supreme who was the victor.

Referring back to the Southern Centre, the Blackmore Vale Club was certainly very busy, organizing meetings at Cannfield in May, June, July, August and two in September. The event on 1 September was the Centre Championship. The admission charge for the meeting was 1s including tax, while parking charges were: cars 1s, motor-cycles 6d and pedal cycles 3d. Prior to September, the track records for four laps of the Cannfield circuit were: (solos) Leslie Jones, 2min 37sec; (sidecars) Stan Hailwood, 3min 4.4sec; (pre-1935 solo) the late Paddy Cash, 2min 33.4secs.

1935 Roll Of Honour

Brands Hatch Championships
250cc – A.H. Castle
350cc – Wally Lock
Individual – Jock West
Sidecar – Brian Ducker

South-Eastern Centre Championships
175cc – H.C. Woodman
250cc – A.H. Castle
350cc – Les Schwieso
Individual – Jock West
Sidecar – W.J. Nethercott

Worcestershire Championship
Bob Foster

Cornish Championships
Eustace, W. Vivian and Huddy & Kneebone Cups – Ivan Kessell
500cc Phillips Cup – Bob Collins
Morcum Shield – Bill Willmott

Worcester, Harrison & Smith Cup
Richie Reynolds

Worcester Jubilee Challenge Trophy
Ivor Webb

Yorkshire Championship
J.H. Reynolds

Southern Centre Championships
350cc and 500cc Experts Barred – Bingley Cree
Unlimited – Ron Evemy
350cc – George Butcher
Sidecar – Tommy Bounds
Central Shield – Ringwood

Swansea Championship
Eddie Thomas

Worcester Auto Club Grand Prix
Fred Lewis

Sydenham & Biggin Hill Championships
175cc – R.G. Hunt
250cc – R.Briscoe
350cc and Matchless Cup – Les Schwieso
Sidecar – George Taylor

Hereford Grand Prix
Tom Loughor

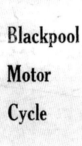

Blackpool   **and Light**

Motor   **Car Club**

Cycle   **Ltd.**

(Affiliated to the Auto-Cycle Union, through the North-Western Centre)

GRASS TRACK
RACES

(Under the General Competition Rules of the A.C.U.)

The Stadium, Squires Gate, Blackpool

ON

SUNDAY, AUGUST 18th, 1935,

Commencing 2-30 p.m.   Price 1d.

OFFICIALS OF THE MEETING:

CLERK OF THE COURSE AND SECRETARY OF MEETING	- C. LAW
TIMEKEEPER AND RESULT STEWARD	- - L. S. CONSTABLE
TREASURER - - - - - -	- W. T. DEWHURST
COMPETITORS' STEWARD - - - -	- G. MORRISON
A.C.U. STEWARD - - - - -	A. TAYLOR

" Gazette & Herald." Blackpool.

Blackpool programme, 1935.

PRICE 2D.

WORCESTER AUTO CLUB

AFFILIATED TO THE WESTERN CENTRE A.C.U

Official Programme

OF A

Grass Track Meeting

TO BE HELD UNDER THE G.C.R. OF THE A.C.U. AT

Rose Place Meadow, Droitwich Road,

WORCESTER,

Sunday Afternoon, June 30th, 1935

Commencing 2.45 p.m.

THE OFFICIALS.

Secretary of Meeting : CLAUDE FISCHER

Stewards : G. H. GOODALL, A.C.U. to be appointed

Starters and Results : E. RODWAY, S. SPRING

Entrance : A. TIDBALL, K. GRAINGER, R. FISCHER

Parking : I. BOUGHTON, R. PRICE,

Programmes : B. BELCHER

Course Stewards : H. NASH, L. BAYLIS

Competitor's Enclosure : W. A. GOODALL

Medical Assistance : WORCESTER V.A.D.

TO SPECTATORS :

The Track is well roped off to ensure your safety, **please do keep outside** and do not sit on the grass inside. The Club and/or its officials cannot accept any liability for injury or loss or damage to property.

NEW MEMBERS INVITED. Join us now and get the most out of your motor-cycling. Membership open to all motor-cycle and light car owners. Remember there is more than one side to motor-cycling—and we cater for everyone—Grass Track Racing—Trials—and also the Social Side of the Sport—If you are a motor-cyclist you will definitely gain by becoming a member of the Worcester Auto Club. The General Secretary is :

Reg. Tidball, 191 Bilford Road, Worcester.

—Come up and see him sometime—

STREETS (PRINTERS) LIMITED, SIDBURY, WORCESTER

Worcester programme, 1935.

10
GRASS-TRACK RACING
1936

The opening event of the season at Ashford Speedway saw Les Schwieso get off to a flying start, when he won the Leith Cup at a meeting organized by the Ashford Kent Motor Club. Also in Kent, two meetings were held at Sittingbourne Football Club, one on 20 May and the other on 17 June. At the former, Eric Oliver (346cc AJS) emerged as the winner of the Unlimited Grand Prix Handicap.

In June, the Taunton Motor Club held a meeting at Shoreditch Farm, South Road in Taunton, where the riders included Ivan Kessell, Reg Beer, Broncho Slade and Tommy Kessell. The Basingstoke and Andover Clubs combined to run one of several meetings that were staged at Winchester Road, Basingstoke.

Poole's Jack Leonard won the 350cc Championship at Brands Hatch and followed up this achievement by winning a Brands Silver Star on a borrowed machine. Silver Stars were highly coveted and were only awarded to competitors who attained a speed of 50mph at the Kent circuit.

Some interesting highlights of the year included Highworth's Roger Wise winning the Evesham Club's Tim Robbins Cup, having achieved the highest aggregate points total throughout the season; Tommy Crutcher, later to ride for Exeter Speedway, starting his grass career; and Wilmot Evans, racing a Triumph, breaking the track record at the Lilleshall circuit.

Pioneer Australian speedway international Billy 'Cyclone' Lamont made a racing appearance at Rocky Park in St Austell. In the East Midlands, the Leicester Query Motor Club were holding meetings, with speedway ace Wilf Plant winning the 500cc event in June. The same Leicester Club would later go on to run the National Championships in the 1950s.

There weren't so many grass-tracks in Scotland, but there was still a reasonable number of meetings organized by the following clubs – Glasgow Motor-Cycle Club, Dunfermline & District Motor-Cycle Club, and Perth & District Motor-Cycle Club. Scottish Speedway star Drew McQueen (Rudge) was a regular winner at the Glasgow-based events.

At Raven Meadow, Worcester, it was Reg Lambourne who was the star man, winning the Sidecar event on a 700cc Brough Superior. Meanwhile, the Solos were dominated by H. French (Rudge), who was triumphant in both the 500cc and Unlimited events.

Welsh ace Roy Zeal had more success in 1936, as he travelled north from his Newport home to win the main finals at the Builth Wells Carnival grass-track.

The Leatherhead & District Motor Club were running meetings at Randalls Park Speedway, while in Herefordshire, the Wye Valley Auto Club staged events at King's Acre in Hereford.

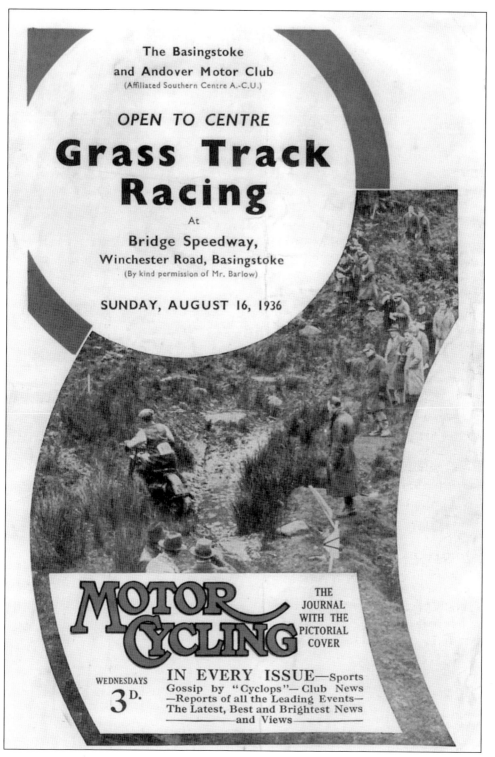

The Basingstoke
and Andover Motor Club
(Affiliated Southern Centre A.-C.U.)

OPEN TO CENTRE

Grass Track Racing

At

Bridge Speedway,
Winchester Road, Basingstoke
(By kind permission of Mr. Barlow)

SUNDAY, AUGUST 16, 1936

MOTOR CYCLING

THE
JOURNAL
WITH THE
PICTORIAL
COVER

WEDNESDAYS
3 D.

IN EVERY ISSUE—Sports
Gossip by "Cyclops"—Club News
—Reports of all the Leading Events—
The Latest, Best and Brightest News
and Views

Bridge Speedway programme, 1936.

Tommy Deadman leads George Buck at Maxstoke.

Cyril Page in spectacular action at Maxstoke.

The Blackmore Vale Motor-Cycle Club ran another full season of racing at Cannfield Speedway in Shaftesbury. In their programme for 26 April, a full line-up of star riders included Mike Erskine, Bingley Cree, Reg Stainer, Jack Leonard and the Hayden brothers, Charlie and Herby. The raceday programme listed the four-lap track records at the venue, as at the end of the previous season: (solos) the late Paddy Cash, 2min 33.4sec; (sidecars) Stan Hailwood, 3min 4.4sec. Incidentally, Stan Hailwood was the father of future Formula One racing driver, Mike. One of the awards at Cannfield during this year included the Browning Trophy, which was presented to the novice or expert-barred rider who achieved the fastest time of the day. Also in 1936, there was a special event entitled the Leonard Cup, which was raced for throughout the season.

The Nantwich & District Motor Club ran a grass-track meeting on 13 July, when Bill Evans won both the 350cc and Unlimited titles. Meanwhile, Vic Challinor took the 500cc event and the First Knock-out, with the Second Knock-out going to Tommy Deadman. Later on in the year (16 August), Vic Challinor won the 350cc final, and Syd 'Skid' Plevin took the 500cc event. The All-Star event saw Jack Wilkinson triumph, while other notable competitors included Jack Gordon, Harold Jackson and Alf Briggs. A further event on 30 September, saw Wilkinson, Jackson and Plevin (two wins) take the honours.

In the London area, the Dons Motor Club held meetings at the Old Rectory Grounds, Fair Lane in Chipstead. At their July event, two of the winners were R. Harris (Solos) and W. Bright (Sidecars). Further to the south-east, the Stonar Football ground at Sandwich played host to grass-track racing as part of the Sandwich Fayre on 13 August.

In the Midlands, knock-out grass mountain races were held at Rushmere Hill, Bridgnorth. Organized by Cygnet (Bridgnorth) Motor-Cycle Club, event one was a match-race team competition between Rushmere, Lilleshall and Wroughton, the three premier mountain-type circuits of the era.

One famous venue that began as a grass speedway track in 1936 was Holbeach. Known as Bell End Speedway, due to the fact that locals reckoned it was the furthest place from which you could actually hear the church bells, the circuit could be found at Whaplode St Catherine, Holbeach, near Spalding in Lincolnshire. Promoted by Holbeach & Spalding Motor-Cycle and Light Car Club, the meetings were organized along speedway lines, with grass straights and shale sprinkled on the bends. Events were run at the circuit until 1939, and again after the war, from 1945. The track finally closed sometime during 1948, apparently due to increasing demands from the farmer who owned the field in which it was situated.

The Ace (Coventry) Motor-Cycle Club organized meetings at Marton-Princethorpe, near Coventry, on a third-of-a-mile circuit with three steep gradients and three tricky downhill slopes. At Worcester in June, it was Northampton's Harry Bowler who won the ten-lap Grand Prix final ahead of Richie Reynolds and Reg Lambourne. Bowler also won the Unlimited final, while Reg Lambourne was triumphant in the 350cc event, and Reynolds emerged victorious in the 500cc event. Meanwhile, the Unlimited Locals Class was won by Fred Lewis.

Many of the tracks in these early years were large oval or mountain-type circuits, but the Evesham Club's Fish Inn Meadow venue at Broadway was just 250 yards in length

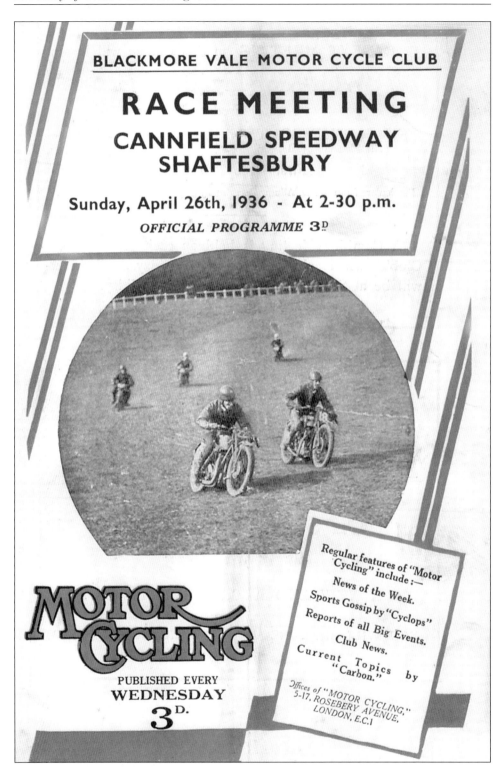

Cannfield programme, 1936.

D O N S
MOTOR CLUB

Hon. Sec. : W. J. MARLEY, 11, Strathleven Road, S.W.2

GRASS TRACK
RACE MEETING

AT

The Old Rectory Grounds
Fair Lane, Chipstead

ON

Sunday, July 5th, 1936

Price 6d. **Programme** Price 6d.

OFFICIALS :

Clerk of the Course	A. E. OWEN
Judge	A. E. BAILEY
Starter	W. J. MARLEY
Handicapper	G. GOLDFINCH
Time-keeper	T. RICHBELL
Paddock Marshals	E. REVILLE, D. BURROWS, J. BURROWS
Gate Marshal	D. T. COGGAN

Chipstead programme, 1936.

– smaller than some of the 1960s Herefordshire Showground circuits.

It was interesting that during these formative years the clubs worked together – one example is the meeting at Cannfield that took place on 1 June, organized by a Southern Combine of Blackmore Vale and Salisbury. The Cannfield venue was later to hold that year's Southern Centre Championship on 27 September. The other two clubs in the Southern Combine (Ringwood and Salisbury) ran at Midgham Speedway, near Ringwood and at Odstock Road in Salisbury.

Also of interest was an advert in a programme stating that the Centre Championships were to be held at Bridge Speedway, Winchester Road in Basingstoke. This poses the question as to where the Centre Championships actually took place – were they held at Cannfield or Basingstoke? Although the choice of venue has become shrouded in mystery, there is no doubt that the individual Champion at this meeting proved to be Ken Goffe.

The Yorkshire Centre Championship was run by Scarborough Motor-Cycle Club on 22 August, with Jack Hargreaves taking victory ahead of Norman Hargreaves, while W. Greenwood was third.

Finally, for 1936, the Midland magazine *Motor Cycle Sport*, named Roger Wise as Champion of the Midlands.

1936 Roll Of Honour

Worcestershire Championship
Roger Wise

South-Eastern Centre Championships
175cc – R.G. Hunt
250cc – S.H. Goddard
350cc – Les Schwieso
650cc – Jock West
Sidecar 500cc – George Taylor
Sidecar 650cc – Arthur Horton
Club – Sidcup

Bucks Championship
Archie Windmill

Shrops & West Midland Show
350cc – Jack Wilkinson
600cc and Unlimited – J.R. Meredith

Salisbury Championship
Solo – R. Biddiscombe
Sidecar – Stuart Waycott

Rochester & Chatham Miers Court Championship
Bill Merrett

South Birmingham Wilcox Cup
G. Wilcox

Aces (Coventry) T.G. Johns Trophy
Tommy Deadman

Sittingbourne Unlimited Grand Prix Championship
Eric Oliver

Southern Centre Championships
Individual – Ken Goffe
Team – Ringwood

Yorkshire Centre Championship
Jack Hargreaves

Biggin Hill Championships
250cc – R. Briscoe
350cc and 500cc – Les Schwieso
Sidecar – G.H. Taylor

Brands Hatch Championships
250cc – W.F. Cullingham
350cc – Les Schweiso
Solo – Tom Arter
Sidecar – Arthur Horton

Fishponds & District Motor Cycle Club.

GRASS TRACK RACES
(CLOSED TO CLUB)

SUNDAY, AUGUST 23rd, 1936.

EVENTS. Unlimited Class.
250 O.H.V. and 350 s.v. Class.
350 O.H.V. and 500 s.v. Class.
Unlimited Class.
Handicap on Cubic Capacity of Engine.
Handicap on Performance.
Class for Competitors Unplaced in Previous Classes.

	Competitors.			*Machine*
1.	D. YOUNG			Humber
2.	W. FROST	250	c.c.	A.J.S.
3.	R. MORGAN	493	,,	B.S.A.
4.	C. SANDERS	349	,,	A.J.S.
5.	F. SHEPHERD	196	,,	Coventry Eagle
6.	B. W. HARRIS	250	,,	New Imperial
7.	S. LANFEAR	499	,,	Rudge
8.	R. BELL	247	,,	Excelsior
9.	A. HEMMINGS	490	,,	Norton
10.	P. M. BULL	490	,,	Norton
11.	B. THOMPSON	250	,,	Coventry Eagle
12.	D. GARDINER	247	,,	Excelsior
14.	F. CHARD	350	,,	Velocette
15.	I. BAILEY	250	,,	Royal Enfield
16.	E. GRIFFITHS	248	,,	Manxman
17.	J. W. LEWIS	350	,,	Douglas
18.	H. S. PHILLIPS	247	,,	Cotton
19.	M. PALMER	500	,,	Ariel
20.	N. KELLY	250	,,	Sunbeam

CLUB SUBSCRIPTION : 4s. 6d. per annum.

Hon. Sec.—M. PALMER, 1a, Cheapside Street, Totterdown.

Fishponds programme, 1936.

Start-line action from Lilleshall.

Billy Lamont, who rode at St Austell in 1936.

John Humphries leads Tommy Deadman at Maxstoke.

Devizes programme, 1936.

FOUNDED 1928

(Affiliated to the S.E. Centre of the A.C.U.)

Hon. Sec.
E. R. Walker, 3, Addington Road, Sittingbourne.

GRASS TRACK MEETING

Held under A.C.U. permit on

Sittingbourne Football Ground, WEDNESDAY, MAY 20th, 1936 at 6.30 p.m.

OFFICIALS

Stewards. H. Jezzard and C. Littlewood
Clerk of the Course and Hon. Sec. of the meeting—

G. EASTON

Sittingbourne programme, 1936.

Brands Hatch programme, 1936.

PROGRAMME

OF

GRASS TRACK RACING

AT THE

FOOTBALL GROUND

Stonar,
SANDWICH

(by kind permission of Sevenscore Estates, Ltd.)

ON

Thur, 13th Aug.

FIRST RACE: 5.30 p.m.

HELD IN CONNECTION WITH

SANDWICH FAYRE

1936

IN AID OF LOCAL
CHARITIES

PROGRAMME . . . . . **PRICE 3d.**

ADAMS PRINTERS, DOVER

Sandwich programme, 1936.

11
GRASS-TRACK RACING
1937

It was announced in April 1937 that the Swindon Works Motor Club was to hold six mountain grass-track events at Manners Farm in Wroughton. Good prize money was on offer for the competitors at the 600-yard circuit and Wroughton Speedway, as it was known, went on to become one of the major success stories of the year. Race meetings were staged on 25 April, 6 June, 20 June, 18 July, 15 August and 19 September. For the latter event, a special souvenir programme was produced, which included pictures and profiles of both riders and officials. A Wroughton Speedway Supporters' Club was formed and a float was entered in the local hospital carnival. With the season being such a triumph, a seventh meeting was organized in aid of local charities. A whole host of 1930s stars won finals at the venue, including Chris Stagg, Bob Foster, Roger Wise, Gerald Selby, Freddie Hudson, Wilmot Evans and Charlie Hayden. Jack 'The Flyer' Williams from Cheltenham, was victorious in the Grand Prix, while the Great Western Trophy went to Roger Wise. Meanwhile, sidecar victors at the circuit included Tommy Bounds and Charlie Bower. Team racing also took place, with two results being:- Wroughton 30, Ringwood 24, and Wroughton 32, South of England 22.

The south was not all about Wroughton, however, with top-class meetings also being held at Layham's Farm in the south-east, and Cannfield in the Southern Centre, among many others in 1937. At Layham's Farm, the fastest average for the lap record was, at one point, held by Les Schwieso, who clocked an impressive speed of 46.87mph.

Grass-track racing was booming in the south, and this was borne out by some of the attendance figures recorded: 7,000 at Cannfield; 3,500 at Wroughton; 2,500 at California (sandtrack); and 2,500 at Salisbury.

In the Midlands, it was the same story, with meetings run at Raven Meadow (Worcester), King's Norton, Redditch, Coventry and Rushmere (South Birmingham). The latter achieved a record attendance of 5,250 for their May meeting, which was combined with a hill climb and actually took place on Whit Monday. The rider of the day was Highworth's Roger Wise, who took victory in the 350cc and Unlimited finals, defeating the midlanders on their own turf. Coventry's Wilmot Evans was second in both races, but he did have a win in the 250cc final. G.L. Buck from Walsall, and Charlie Bower of Birmingham were the Sidecar winners.

In the west country, racing took place on a monthly basis at Holway Hill, Taunton in Somerset. Among the riders that excelled at these events were Roy Zeal, Stan Lanfear, Reg Beer, Broncho Slade, Vic Worlock, Bert Jones and Jack Leonard, but the rider who became the star of Taunton was Cornwall's Ivan Kessell.

Down in the south-east, the sidecar racing was very exciting, with the major battles taking place between Eric Oliver, Brian Ducker and Jack Surtees. That said, though, the

Oxford Motor-Cycle Speedway Club

Headquarters:

THE MAGDALEN ARMS HOTEL, IFFLEY ROAD,
OXFORD.

2d. Programme 2d.

of

Grass Track Racing

at

SANDFORD-ON-THAMES

on

SUNDAY, AUGUST 22nd, 1937,

at 2.30 p.m.

Dont miss our=====NEXT EVENT

which will be on

SUNDAY, SEPTEMBER 5th, at 2.30.

Oliver & Son, Printers, 73 George Street, Oxford.

Sandford-on-Thames programme, 1937.

Number 23, Wilmot Evans, leads Jack Booker (36) and Roger Wise.

solos had a very big following, with the ace riders including Wally Lock, Tom Arter, Bill Hallett, George Rayner, Don Arter and Roy Craighead.

All over Britain, grass-track racing could be watched, with clubs and events including Chalfont & Amersham Auto Club at Denham in Buckinghamshire; the Brands Hatch Combine events, which boasted crowds of 5,000 to 10,000; Basingstoke & Hants Motor Club; Sydenham Motor Club (Layham's Farm); Brighton & District Motor-Cycle Club; King's Norton (Weatheroak Bank); Worcester Auto Club (Raven Meadow); Evesham (Crown Meadow); Leicester; Birmingham (Lilleshall); Nantwich (Cheshire); Moseley & District Motor-Cycle Club; Chester Mountain Grass-track; Ilkeston (Derbyshire); Fishponds (Bristol); Barham (Kent); Swansea; North Cornwall (Launceston). This list covers just some of the many that were running at the time.

1937 was a good year for the Nantwich Club, and they were thought of as the premier northern grass-track club. Some of the stars who appeared during the year included Bill Evans, Jack Wilkinson, Vic Challinor, Syd 'Skid' Plevin, Geoff Godwin and Les Graham.

The established England speedway international and Belle Vue rider, Bill Kitchen, returned to the grass on 27 June at Nantwich, winning two special challenge races against the locals. Bill also broke the lap record for the circuit in the process, while the best of the rest was Vic Challinor, who won two of the Unlimited finals. It is not wished to diminish Challinor's achievements, but his two final triumphs did not feature Kitchen as an opponent. Challinor did, however, collect a few scalps to boast of, including Bill Evans, Andy Mackay, Les Graham, Harry Terretta, Jack Gordon, Geoff Godwin, plus future speedway aces Jack D. White (who appeared for both Belle Vue and Sheffield after the war) and Albert 'Aussie' Rosenfeld, who later died ten days after crashing at the Odsal Stadium, Bradford on 6 July 1946.

Kitchen again rode at Nantwich on 8 August, breaking his own lap record and winning a special challenge event. The other finals that Kitchen did not contest were won by another speedway rider, Oliver Hart. There was also sidecar racing at the venue, with notable competitors including Charlie Wickman and Frank 'Digger' Eastwick. In September, Kitchen's lap record was broken by F. Kenyon, with Bill only managing third place in a special challenge.

Sticking with the Nantwich Club, their most notable venue was at Birchall Moss Farm, Hatherton, close to Nantwich. The venue was almost directly across the road from Hatherton Hall Farm, the club's famous scrambles circuit, which went on to host national events in the 1950s, 1960s and 1970s.

The prestigious Southern Centre Championships were staged by the Salisbury Club at Odstock, with the Individual event going to Ken Goffe, while Ringwood collected the team title. Full results from Salisbury were:

500cc Championship – First: Ken Goffe, Second: Jack Leonard, Third: Leslie Jones
Unlimited Novice – First: W. Coat, Second: C. Mulhuish, Third: Tom Crutcher
Unlimited Open – First: Leslie Jones, Second: Jack Leonard, Third: Bingley Cree
Unlimited Experts Barred – First: Herby Hayden, Second: Jack Difazio, Third: Reg Stainer
350cc Open – First: Jack Leonard, Second: Leslie Jones, Third: Bingley Cree
Handicap (12 fastest riders) – First: Gerald Selby, Second: Reg Stainer, Third: Jack Difazio

On parade at Rocky Park, including Wilfred Bennetts, Tommy Kessell, Chirpy Richards and Bob Collins.

Wroughton programme, 1937.

First Sidecar – First: Jack Surtees, Second: Stan Bell, Third: Tommy Bounds
Second Sidecar – First: Jack Surtees, Second: Tommy Bounds, Third: Stan Bell

The annual Boscombe Hospital Carnival Fete brought in a crowd of 20,000 people, with many of them watching the grass-track racing on Wednesday 10 August. Astonishingly, a total of fifteen races were run in just one-and-a-quarter hours, with local rider Charlie Hayden doing the double with victories in the 350cc and Unlimited Classes.

In the 1930s and 1940s, Wembley Speedway boasted a huge supporters' club, as well as a Wembley Speedway Sports Motor Club. Regular races took place as part of a Gymkhana and one such event took place on 15 August, in front of 2,000 spectators. The meeting was run on a 440-yard grass circuit and featured a team match between Wembley and Chalfont & Amersham.

Having previously mentioned the Southern Centre Championship, the other big area event of the year was Brands Hatch-staged South-Eastern Championship, which took place on a lovely sunny day in August. In recording an average speed of 46.59mph, Jack Surtees took the Sidecar title, defeating Harold Taylor and W.J. Nethercott. Meanwhile, Les Schwieso won the solo title, clocking an average speed of 51.77mph. Full results from Brands Hatch were:

South-Eastern Championship – First: Les Schwieso, Second: R.A. Scott, Third: Angus Herbert
350cc Class – First: Les Schwieso, Second: Eric Oliver, Third: Angus Herbert
250cc Class – First: Alf Castle, Second: A. Matterface, Third: R. Marsh
Sidecar Championship – First: Jack Surtees, Second: Harold Taylor, Third: W.J. Nethercott
500cc Sidecar – First: Harold Taylor, Second: W.J. Nethercott, Third: Brian Ducker.

Eric Oliver, who later was to become World Sidecar Champion in the 1950s, proved how talented he was by winning a Brands Hatch Silver Star, both in the Solos and the Sidecars, for his 50mph-plus race times.

The Wessex Centre was thriving and clubs in the area that held meetings during the year included Fishponds (Downend and Frenchay, Bristol); North Wilts Motor-Cycle and Light Car Club (Purton and Broome Lane, Swindon); and Swindon Works (Wroughton). There was also the West Wilts Club, which was gearing up for the opening of Farleigh Castle the following year. At their meeting on August Bank Holiday Monday, the victors were: Unlimited & Open finals – Charlie Hayden; Unlimited Novice – Herby Hayden; Unlimited Club final – Jack Difazio; 350cc Class – G. Ray; and 350cc Novice – G. Hale.

Successful meetings were run by the Fishponds Club, and one such event took place at Briarfield Farm, Downend on 26 September, when the victorious competitors were recorded as follows:

350cc Class – First: Colin Mead, Second: Reg Lambourne, Third: H. Phillips
Unlimited final – First: Colin Mead, Second: Roy Zeal, Third: Graham Parry

350cc Open – First: Reg Lambourne, Second: Colin Mead, Third: Roy Zeal
250cc Class – First: H. Phillips, Second: R. Morgan
Handicap – First: H. Phillips, Second: Colin Mead, Third: R. Morgan.

The Welsh Championship was staged at Pontypool on 28 August and saw Richie Reynolds take victory ahead of Roy Zeal and C.W. Boss.

Finally for 1937, an interesting advert appeared for a scheduled meeting at Dundridge Speedway, Bishop's Waltham on 29 August. The meeting was organized by the Albatross Motor-Cycle Club (Southern) for the Hampshire Racing Combine and the advert stated that 'The newest and fastest track in the Southern Centre compares favourably with the famous Cannfield Speedway, with long straights, fast surface and natural grandstand'.

1937 Roll Of Honour

Wroughton Grand Prix
Jack Williams

Eastern Counties Championship
Sam 'Crasher' Warren

Worcestershire Championship
Wilmot Evans

Southern Centre Championships
350cc – Jack Leonard
Individual – Ken Goffe
Sidecar – Jack Surtees
Team – Ringwood

Welsh Championship
Richie Reynolds

Moseley Grand Prix
L. Harrowfield

Boscombe Carnival
350cc and Open – Charlie Hayden
Novice – Herby Hayden
Sidecar – Stan Appleby

South Midland Centre Championships
250cc – C.A. Jenner

350cc – Pete Lansdale
600cc – Cyril Brine
Club – North-East London Motor-Cycle Club

Brands Hatch Championships
250cc – A.H. Castle
350cc and 650cc – Les Schwieso
Sidecar – Jack Surtees

South-Eastern Centre Championships
250cc – Bill Hallett
350cc and 650cc – Les Schwieso
Sidecar – Jack Surtees

Hastings Championships
Solo – Tom Arter
Sidecar – Taffy Graham

Sydenham & Layhams Championships
250cc – R. Briscoe
350cc – Les Schwieso
Unlimited – Jock West
500cc and Unlimited Sidecar – W. Graham

Great Western Trophy
Roger Wise

Nantwich Challenge Cup
D. Dunn

Tim Robbins Challenge Cup
Wilmot Evans

Lincolnshire Championship
Ted English

12
GRASS-TRACK RACING
1938

The second year of the famous Wroughton Speedway produced another six top-class meetings, before the Air Ministry took over the land. Jack Williams was still the man to beat at Wroughton, as he emerged triumphant in the Great Western Trophy, finishing ahead of Roger Wise. Other winners at the circuit in '38 included Wilmot Evans, Doug Perks, Andy MacKay and Ken Witts, while some team events resulted thus: Wroughton 22, Midland Aces 31; Wroughton 35, Ringwood 19; Wroughton 33, Rushmere 21; Wroughton 28, Lilleshall 26. The home side's skipper was Roger Wise, who, incidentally, was the brother of the public relations officer and track announcer, Reg. The club also had a tortoise called 'Joey', who filled the position of team mascot and even had his shell painted in the team's colours of green and yellow.

All the top riders from the Southern, Midland and Wessex Centre areas raced at Wroughton, and as well as the winners previously listed above, these included: Oliver Bevan, Chris Stagg, Gerald Selby, Ted Commander, Tommy Wood, Dick Tolley, Freddie Hudson, Fred Philpotts, Stan Lanfear, Jack Difazio, David Floyd and Bert Shorey, father of the 1960s road racer, Dan Shorey.

The Evesham Club ran a mountain grass-track meeting at Fish Inn Meadow, Broadway in Worcestershire on Whit Sunday, 5 June. Roger Wise had a field day, scooping the victor's laurels in three events – 250cc, 350cc and Unlimited finals. This was some feat, as there was a strong Midland line-up for the meeting, which included Eddie Blackwell (Leamington), Tommy Deadman (Wombourne), Andy MacKay (Dudley), Dick Tolley (Worcester) and Wilmot Evans (Coventry).

The day after the Evesham event was the start of something very special in the history of grass-track racing. Just south of Bath, at Farleigh Hungerford, the West Wilts Club organized the first-ever meeting at Farleigh Castle. Mike Erskine designed the track, while the meeting officials included Reg Wise, who was the race commentator, and Vic Anstice, who was the timekeeper. The winner of the very first race at Farleigh was W. Kelly from Melksham. Full results of that historic first meeting were:

Unlimited Novice final – First: J.R. Lewis, Second: E. Gawler, Third: W. Kelly
350cc final – First: Stan Lanfear, Second: Roger Wise
Unlimited final (club members only) – First: Richie Reynolds, Second: Colin Mead, Third: G. Sleightholme
Unlimited final (open) – First: Richie Reynolds, Second: Colin Mead, Third: Roger Wise
Handicap final – First: K.L. Witts, Second: Stan Lanfear, Third: Roger Wise
Fastest six – First: Roger Wise, Second: F.G. Philpotts, Third: Colin Mead.

Wroughton programme, 1938.

The official programme cost 2d and emblazoned on the cover was 'Premier opening meeting of the Farleigh Castle Speedway'. Included in the programme was an advert for a new Ford Eight Motor Car, which could be purchased for £120 from E. Dennis of Castle Street, Trowbridge. The programme also made mention of the West Wilts Supporters' Club, which could be joined for an annual subscription of 1s, and upon becoming a member, half-price entry could be gained to race meetings.

Later on in the season, the Farleigh Castle Grand Prix was held and attracted a crowd of some 4,000 spectators. They witnessed Roger Wise take victory ahead of Bristol's Fred Philpotts and Gloucestershire's Colin Mead.

OFFICIAL PROGRAMME—THREEPENCE

SWINDON WORKS' MOTOR CLUB
(RACING SECTION)

OPEN-TO-CENTRE

MOUNTAIN GRASS TRACK RACE MEETING

(Held under the General Competition Rules of the A.C.U.),

at **WROUGHTON SPEEDWAY**
(by kind permission of Mr. Manners)

on SUNDAY, MAY 15th, 1938

First Race at 2.30

ORGANISING COMMITTEE :
P. ROBINS (Chairman), S. ROGER WISE (Captain), R. F. J. WISE, A. E. BAILEY (Secretary)

OFFICIALS :

A.C.U. Steward	C. H. KING, Esq. (Hon. Secretary, Wessex Centre Board)
Club Steward	I. ROGERS, Esq. (Swindon Works' M.C.)
Judges	W. C. BIZLEY, Esq., Dr. B. R. CROSSLEY, R. THOMPSON, Esq., Dr. BROADFOOT
Hon. Medical Officer	Dr. B. R. CROSSLEY
Starter	WITHIL, Esq.
Paddock Marshals	F. E. B. FELLOWES, Esq., W. NICHOLS, Esq. and N. FISHER, Esq.
Official Timekeeper	V. ANSTICE, Esq., A.C.U. (Chairman, Wessex Centre)
Machine Examiner	H. JARMAN, Esq.
Club Announcer	
Racing Commentator	REG. F. J. WISE
Track Marshals	MEMBERS OF S.W.M.C. (Chief Marshal, A. Porter, Esq.), and WEST WILTS M.C.)
Car Park Marshals	MEMBERS OF SWINDON & DISTRICT M.C. (Chief Marshal, P. Maynard, Esq.)
Groundsman	W. HUFF
Clerk of the Course	P. ROBINS, Esq.
Secretary of Meeting	A. E. BAILEY, Esq., 55, OXFORD ROAD, SWINDON.

Printed by The Swindon Press Ltd., Newspaper House, Swindon, Wilts.

It was still boom-time in the Southern Centre as Salisbury (Odstock), Portsmouth (Dundridge Speedway, Bishop's Waltham), Ringwood (Corfe Mullen Speedway) and Southampton (Totton) were all active in 1938. In the South Midlands Centre, the North Hants Motor Club ran successful meetings at the rather interestingly-named Murrell Green Speedway in Hartley Wintney.

The size and shape of the circuits showed great variance, with some examples being: Cannfield, which was 880 yards in length and included an 's' bend; Corfe Mullen, which was 500 yards long with an 's' bend; Odstock, which was 655 yards in length and had an 's' bend – but while the solos ran in an anti-clockwise direction, the sidecars circumnavigated the course in a clockwise manner.

The prestigious Southern Centre Individual Championship was won by Reg Stainer at Cannfield on 11 September. In the East-South Wales Centre, racing was held by the Pontypool Club at the Polo ground on the Pontypool Road. At the meeting which took place at the end of April, it was Richie Reynolds who dominated with wins in the 350cc, 500cc, Unlimited and Centre Championship races. Reg Lambourne, George Bason and Roy Zeal all featured in the results at Pontypool.

At the other end of the country in Stockport, Vic Challinor was the man to beat, with the Stockport Club running a series of meetings during 1938. In the Tamworth area, the Midland Social Motor-Cycle Club organized meetings, and it was Walter Stanford who emerged victorious at the July event. Walter was, in fact, the father of Bill and Bob, the

OFFICIAL PROGRAMME, Price 2d.

Fishponds & District Motor Cycle Club.

Affiliated to the Auto-Cycle Union through the Wessex Centre, A.-C.U.

GRASS TRACK RACE MEETING

Held under the A.-C.U. General Competition Rules, restricted to members of Clubs in the Wessex Centre, at

HENFIELD SPEEDWAY,

near Westerleigh, on

SUNDAY, MAY 29th, 1938,

First Event 2.30 p.m.

OFFICIALS.

Stewards—Mr. F. W. Wiltshire & Mr. W. Dibsdall.

Clerk of the Course—Mr. F. Hatherall.

Secretary of the Meeting—Mr. G. Reid.

Machine Examiner—Mr. W. Shepherd.

COMPETITORS.

No.	Name	Machine	Town
1	R. Stainer	350 Jap, 500 Rudge	Dorset
2	W. Frost	346 A.J.S.	Bristol
3	S. Tuck	499 Rudge	Bristol
4	B. Butt	499 Rudge	Bristol
5	K. Witts	348 Velo.	Devizes
6	J. Difazio	348 Velo.	Middlesex
7	H. Phillips	172 H.P., 500 H.P., 500 Rudge s/c.	Bristol
8	S. Lanfear	499 Rudge, 348 A.J.S.	Bristol
9	C. Mead	350 & 500 Mead Special	Tewkesbury
10	T. Bounds	596 Norton s/c.	Andover
11	T. Bounds (Rider, E. May)	596 Norton s/c.	Andover
12	H. Jones	500 Douglas	Newport
14	A. Davis	348 O.K. Supreme	Newport
15	P. Hadley	499 Rudge	Dursley
16	W. Kelly	350 J.A.P.	Melksham
17	H. Bracey	348 Calthorpe	Bristol
18	P. Falconer	343 Triumph	Stroud
19	W. Splaine	500 J.A.P.	Bristol
20	H. Webb	348 Rex Acme	Bath
21	F. Cole	500 Rudge	Alveston
22	R. Webb	349 Velo.	Keynsham
23	H. Sweatman	499 Rudge	Sodbury
24	H. Tiley	348 A.J.S.	Sodbury
25	A. Pearce	350——	Devizes
26	R. Zeal	350 J.A.P., 500 Rudge	Newport
27	W. Fry	494 Douglas s/c.	Bristol
28	J. Leonard	350 Miller	Poole
29	T. Crutcher	350 Miller	Poole
30	F. Philpotts	350 Velo.	Bristol
31	G. Parry	500 Rudge	Bristol
32	W. Matthews	500 Rudge	Bristol
33	E. Thorne	250 Velo.	Bristol

H. H. Phillips & Son, Fishponds.

Henfield programme, 1938.

Colin Mead leads at the Worcestershire Championship.

1960s aces from Weedon, near Northampton.

Other meetings in 1938 were held by Coventry & Warwickshire Motor Club (at Maxstoke Castle), Hartlepool and District Motor Club (at Klondyke Speedway, Elwick), Pathfinders Motor-Cycle Club (at Markeaton Park, Derby), Stratford-on-Avon Light Car and Motor-Cycle Club (at Bridgetown Farm), Chester Motor Club, Perth and District Motor-Cycle Club (at South Inch), Leicester Query Motor Club, Wigston Speedway, and by Green Motor-Cycle Club of Twickenham (at Chertsey Bridge).

The Kent area still played host to the two major events of the year, with Brands Hatch staging its own self-titled Championships, while the South-Eastern Championships were held at Layham's Farm. At Brands Hatch, racing started in dusty conditions, with rain arriving later in the proceedings. Wally Lock got the better of Les Schwieso in the 350cc final, although Les was the master of the 650cc final. Detailed results were:

250cc Championship – First: Bill Hallett, Second: F. Lancaster, Third: Don Arter
350cc Championship – First: Wally Lock, Second: Les Schwieso, Third: Bill Hallett
650cc Championship – First: Les Schwieso, Second: Wally Lock, Third: Alf Castle

Other winners were Bill Merrett in the Grand Prix Solo Handicap and Eric Oliver, who took the chequered flag in both the 500cc and 650cc Sidecar finals.

Just over a week later, it was the South-Eastern Centre Championships at Layham's Farm, where Bill Hallett again took the 250cc final, while Les Schwieso became the double champion, winning the 350cc and Unlimited finals. Jack Surtees was triumphant

MOTOR RACING

INCORPORATING SOUTHERN SPEEDWAYS MAGAZINE

PUBLISHED FORTNIGHTLY   **3ᴰ**   APRIL —— OCTOBER

JULY 9th, 1938   Vol. II., No. 13

A. C. Mackay, 346 O.K. Supreme, the new track record holder at Lilleshall Hall (Birmingham M.C.)

Motor Racing *magazine, 9 July 1938.*

INCORPORATING SOUTHERN SPEEDWAYS MAGAZINE

PUBLISHED FORTNIGHTLY 3ᴰ APRIL ——— OCTOBER

SEPTEMBER 3rd, 1938   Vol. II., No. 17

WESTWOOD'S RUSHMERE DOUBLE

T. H. WESTWOOD (500 T.H.W. s/c.), who won both Sidecar events at the South Birmingham M.C's. last meeting at Rushmere.

Motor Racing *magazine, 3 September 1938.*

in the Sidecar Championship, when clocking a super-fast speed of 42.95mph. The results were:

175cc Championship – First: Ken Frogley, Second: E. Cullingham, Third: B. Hall
250cc Championship – First: Bill Hallett, Second: K. Blay, Third: F. Lancaster
350cc Championship – First: Les Schwieso, Second: Bill Merrett, Third: Wally Lock
Unlimited Championship – First: Les Schwieso, Second: Bill Merrett, Third: Eric Oliver

The Layham's Farm venue also hosted the Matchless Cup on 17 July, which saw Jock West take victory in the twenty-lap event on his Hartley Ariel machine. Runner-up was Les Schwieso on a 350cc AJS, while third place went to Bill Merrett (350cc Velo).

As previously mentioned, team racing was very popular during this period, and the Brands Hatch side boasted a very impressive line-up which included: Wally Lock, who started racing in 1932 and went on to win major championships at Brands Hatch and Layham's Farm; Les Schwieso, who also started his motor-cycling career in 1932, and won many titles, including events at both Layham's Farm and Brands Hatch; Alf Castle, who began racing in 1928 and went on to win the 250cc South-Eastern title on three occasions, before moving into the 500cc Class in 1937; and Angus Herbert, whose racing career started in 1928 and who won events at Layham's Farm and Brands Hatch. Every member of the Brands Hatch team had also previously won a Silver Star, for recording speeds in excess of 50mph at the famous Brands circuit.

The other top team of 1938, was the Blackmore Vale side, who raced at Cannfield Speedway in Dorset. They included: Ken Goffe, who came from Reading and started his career at Longmoor Speedway, California in Wokingham; Jack Leonard, from Poole, who began racing in 1928, and was also a Centre Champion; Stan Lanfear, who went on to have a successful speedway career with Sheffield and Plymouth (Stan was from Fishponds in Bristol and was a regular at the Farleigh Castle meetings. He held track records at Cannfield and Salisbury and was known as both 'Speedway Stan' and 'The Wrecker'); and Reg Stainer, who was from West Moors, near Ringwood, and was the 1938 Southern Centre Champion.

A team match was held at Brands Hatch on 24 July, and saw the homesters defeat Blackmore Vale, 20-15. In the Silver Star event that followed, Ken Goffe (Rudge) defeated Jock West (Hartley Ariel).

Although Stan Lanfear became a star when racing for Blackmore Vale in the Southern Centre, he almost didn't have to venture out of the Wessex Centre – just look at this fixture list for the area in 1938:

24 April – Swindon Works (Wroughton)
15 May – Swindon Works
29 May – Fishponds (Henfield Speedway, Westerleigh)
6 June – West Wilts (Farleigh Castle)
19 June – Swindon Works
26 June – Fishponds
3 July – Swindon Works

Sandford programme.

9 July – Fishponds
10 July – West Wilts
16 July – Shepton Mallet (Cannards Grave)
20 July – Bristol Motor-Cycle & Light Car Club (Mountain Grass-track, Whitchurch)
23 July – Fishponds
31 July – West Wilts
7 August – Shepton Mallet
14 August – Swindon Works
21 August – Fishponds
28 August – West Wilts
4 September – Fishponds
18 September – Swindon Works
2 October – Swindon Works.

NEXT RACE MEETING—SUNDAY, OCTOBER 2nd, at 2.30 p.m.

Oxford Motor-Cycle Speedway Club
(Affiliated to the South Midland Centre. A.C.U.)

2d. Official Programme 2d.
OF
Grass Track Racing
at
SANDFORD-ON-THAMES
on
SUNDAY, SEPT. 18th, 1938, at 3 p.m.
Held under the General Competition Rules of the Auto-Cycle Union. Permit No. R. 979.

FAULKNER for your Motor-Cycle

Whatever make or type of machine you require, Faulkner is fairly certain to have it.
Whether your choice is New, or Second-hand, Faulkner can fix you up.
However small your income, Faulkner can arrange payments to suit it.
Why deny yourself the pleasure of motor-cycling ?
Get in touch with Faulkner right away !
Faulkner offers you a really straightforward deal, and the fairest and most helpful treatment it is possible to obtain.

12 Cardigan Street, :: Oxford.

Oliver & Son, Printers, 73 George Street, Oxford.

There was good promotion of the sport in the 1930s, with the West Wilts Grass-track Committee organizing floats for the carnivals at both Devizes and Trowbridge. Swindon Works also entered a float in their local carnival, and they had a sign-written van that advertised their race meetings. Both of these go-ahead organizations also ran supporters' clubs for their fans to join.

As far as regular meetings were concerned, it was a similar story in the Southern Centre, with events being staged almost every week. The most popular of the organizing clubs were: Ringwood (at Corfe Mullen Speedway), Salisbury (at Odstock), Blackmore Vale (at Cannfield), and the Hampshire Combine meetings.

Team racing was not just restricted to Blackmore Vale, Brands Hatch, St Austell, Lilleshall, Wroughton and Farleigh Castle, for some of the smaller clubs also held team events. One example came in September, when the Worcester Auto Club's meeting at Raven Meadow on the Droitwich Road incorporated a Worcester *v.* Oxford match. For this event, Worcester were represented by Colin Mead, Richie Reynolds, Reg Lambourne, Fred Lewis, Roy Zeal, Dick Tolley and Jim Cashmore. Regular team racing was also held between Oxford and Reading, with the former racing at Sandford-on-Thames, while the latter rode at Longmoor Speedway in California. Some of the team results from the year included: Farleigh Castle 30, Wroughton 24; Holbeach & Spalding 60, Ringwood 48; Brands Hatch 21, Blackmore Vale 15; and Cannfield 28, Brands Hatch 8.

Some of the other circuits used in 1938 included: Taunton, which was quarter of a mile in length and oval-shaped, with natural banking and Fishponds, which was a 400-yard oval circuit with a slight gradient. In the south-east, the Leatherhead Club held their events at Randalls Park, which included several bends, one of which was a hairpin, and the Hartley Wintney Motor Club used a 400-yard oval-shaped track. However, despite being based in Hampshire, the club has affiliated to the South Midlands centre.

The Midland tracks at Rushmere and Lilleshall were mountain-type circuits, which resembled scrambles tracks. Both of these circuits, along with Wroughton, took part in a mountain grass-track team league during the course of the year.

1938 Roll Of Honour

Great Western Trophy
Jack Williams

Wroughton Grand Prix
Roger Wise

Southern Centre Championships
350cc and 600cc – Jack Leonard
Individual – Reg Stainer
Sidecar – Jack Surtees

Brands Hatch Championships
250cc – Bill Hallett
350cc – Wally Lock
650cc – Les Schwieso
Grand Prix Solo Handicap – Bill Merrett
500cc And 650cc Sidecar – Eric Oliver

Worcestershire Championship
Colin Mead

South-Eastern Centre Championships
175cc – Ken Frogley
250cc – Bill Hallett
350cc and Unlimited – Les Schwieso
Sidecar – Jack Surtees

Barham Solo Championship
Tom Arter

100 Guineas Challenge Cup (Layham's Farm)
Jock West

Tim Robbins Challenge Cup (Evesham)
Roger Wise

Pontypool & East-South Wales Championship
Richie Reynolds

West Wilts Opening Event (Farleigh Castle)
Novice – J.R. Lewis
Handicap – Ken Witts
350cc – Stan Lanfear
Unlimited – Richie Reynolds

Matchless Cup (Layham's Farm)
Jock West

13
GRASS-TRACK RACING
1939

This was to be the final year of grass-track's steady growth in the United Kingdom. It was a wonderful year for grass fans, but it was due to come to almost a full stop with the outbreak of the Second World War in September.

In the Wessex Centre, the now prestigious titles went to exciting local rider Vic Worlock in the 500cc class, while Swindon's Roger Wise took the 350cc title. Based on present-day standards, Roger would be classed as an all-round superstar, as he was top of his class in grass-track circles. Roger also had a successful career with the Bristol Bulldogs Speedway side, as well as riding in sidecar trials and reaching the top in scrambles, winning the big National Cotswold Scramble Championship. Returning to the Wessex Championships of 1939, the Sidecar title went to Eric Oliver, the 'King of Brands'.

A popular venue this year, was the Crown Speedway at Tolldown, situated on the eastern side of Bristol. This circuit was around 600 yards in length, with an 's' bend, and hosted regular monthly race meetings during the season. Riders who raced at Crown Speedway included Ken Witts, Vic Worlock, Graham Parry, Jack Difazio, Newport's Herbie Jones and Harry Bamford from Hanham in Bristol, who rode Douglas and Rudge machines.

Swindon Works Motor-Cycle Club and West Wilts at Farleigh Castle were still very popular, while another venue opened on 7 May, at Swainswick Speedway, which was situated three miles from Bath at Down Farm on the A46 Gloucester Road. Meetings at the new one-mile, pear-shaped circuit were organized by the Bath and West Motor Club, who charged the public an admission price of 6d.

Looking at the *Southern Centre Gazette No.95* for February 1939, what an impressive fixture list there was in the South:

10 April –Salisbury
16 April – Ringwood
23 April – Blackmore Vale
30 April – Southampton
7 May – Salisbury
14 May – Ringwood
21 May – Southampton
28 May – Blackmore Vale
4 June – Hants Combine
11 June – Salisbury
18 June – Ringwood

Mike Erskine, setting the grass alight.

Ivan Kessell in full flight.

Farleigh Castle programme, 1939.

OFFICIAL PROGRAMME, 3D.

East Midland Centre, A.-C.U.

GRASS TRACK RACES

Alton Towers

Sunday, 7th May, 1939

2.45 p.m.

MOTOR CYCLING

Regular features of
"Motor Cycling" include:—
News of the Week.
Sports Gossip by "Cyclops"
Reports of all Big Events.
Club News.
Current Topics by
"Carbon."

Edited by
GRAHAM WALKER

PUBLISHED EVERY WEDNESDAY

3D.

Alton Towers programme, 1939.

25 June – Blackmore Vale
2 July – Southampton
9 July – Ringwood
16 July – Hants Combine
23 July – Blackmore Vale
30 July – Salisbury
7 August – Ringwood
13 August – Southampton
20 August – Blackmore Vale
27 August – Salisbury
3 September – Ringwood
10 September – Centre Championships
17 September – Blackmore Vale
24 September – Salisbury
1 October – Southampton

Mentioning some of the Southern Centre circuits, Ringwood Club events took place at Corfe Mullen, some three miles from Wimborne, on a 500-yard track with an 's' bend. Meanwhile, the Blackmore Vale Club ran at Cannfield, which featured an 880-yard circuit with an 's' bend, plus a climb and descent. The prize money at the Blackmore Vale finals ranged from £3 to £5. Salisbury race meetings were held at Odstock Road, East Harnham on a 655-yard track, again with an 's' bend. Sidecars circumnavigated the course in a clockwise direction, while the solos took an anti-clockwise route. Southampton Motor Club, meanwhile, used a grass speedway circuit on the Totton to Salisbury Road.

Champion for 1939 was the Australian Bert Jones, who used to live near Newquay. The former Cornish Champion also enjoyed a successful time with Southampton Speedway. While on the subject of Southampton Speedway, future Saints and Wembley ace Charlie May started riding on the grass in 1939. Charlie's son, Richard, was to become a top grass-tracker in the 1960s, before going on to fame with Reading Speedway.

Probably due to the clouds of war looming on the horizon, the Centre Championships were brought forward and actually took place at Salisbury Speedway on 30 July. The results were:

Unlimited final – First: Bert Jones (Jap), Second: Stan Lanfear (Rudge), Third: C. Holt (Rudge)
Open final – First: Bert Jones (Jap), Second: Ken Goffe (Rudge), Third: Gerald Selby (Rudge)
350cc final – First: Jack Leonard (Velo), Second: Gerald Selby (Jap), Third: C. Holt (Rudge)
Sidecar final – First: Tommy Bounds (Norton), Second: Stan Bell (Excelsior), Third: E.H. May (Ariel)

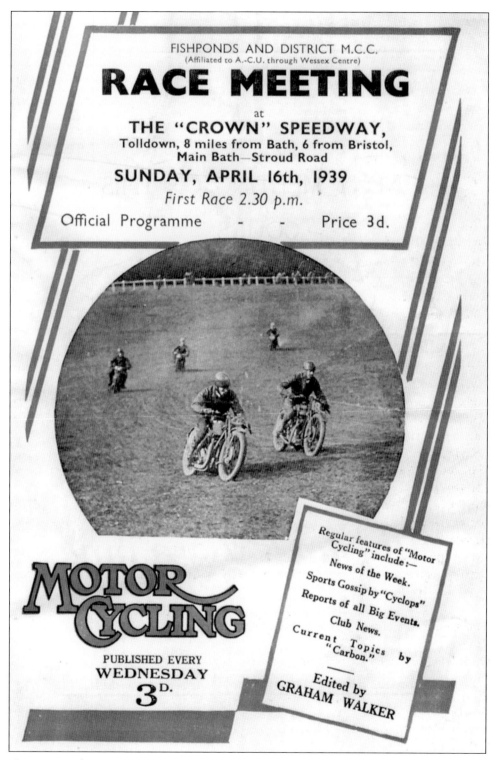

Crown speedway programme, 1939.

OFFICIAL PROGRAMME   PRICE 2d.

Bath & West of England M.C.
(Affiliated Wessex Centre A.C.U.)

SWAINSWICK SPEEDWAY

GRAND OPENING MEETING

SUNDAY, MAY 7th 1939

OPEN TO CENTRE EVENT

OFFICIALS OF THE MEETING.

Wessex A.C.U. Steward: C. H. King, Esq.
Club Steward: S. Hughes, Esq.
Timekeeper: V. Anstice, A.C.U.
Starter and Flag Marshal: F. Lee, Esq.
Machine Examiners and Competitors Stewards:
R. Medway, Esq. and E. A. Thomas, Esq.
Secretary of Meeting:
H. C. Croft, Esq., Windsor Service Station, Lower Weston, Bath.
Phone: 7420.
Organising Committee:
Messrs. F. J. Lee, S. Hughes, V. Anstice, E. Thomas, R. Medway,
and H. C. Croft.

Cigarettes, Chocolates, Fruit, Ices, Etc., on sale in the
Grounds.

Swainswick programme, 1939.

Sidecar action from Lilleshall.

The Blackmore Vale team at Farleigh Castle on 18 June 1939, including Ken Goffe,
Jack Oifazio, Stan Lanfear and Jack Leonard.

Ringwood took the Club Shield from Blackmore Vale, Southampton, Salisbury, Weymouth, Bishop's Waltham, Waterlooville and Chichester, in that order.

Before looking at other areas away from the Wessex and Southern Centre, on 16 July, the Swindon Works Motor Club, who were then running at Avebury Speedway, played host to the Blackmore Vale team, with the visitors securing a 20-16 victory. Representing the victorious Blackmore Vale team were Reg Stainer (captain), Stan Lanfear, Gerald Selby and Jack Difazio, while the Swindon side was made up by Roger Wise (captain), Ivan Kessell, Reg Lambourne and Vic Worlock. Both Jack Difazio and Stan Lanfear recorded 9-point maximums for the winning side.

The 680-yard Avebury circuit was a popular venue and received entries from London, Cornwall, Worcestershire, Wales and Oxfordshire, plus the regulars from the Wessex and Southern Centre areas for the meetings it hosted.

Further north, the Halifax Club organized meetings at the Old Earth Rugby field in Elland, while down in the south-west, Plymouth organized what they termed a grass-track scramble at Modbury. Other meetings in the Plymouth area were staged at Heathfield Manor, with the Slee brothers (Ben and Ken) and Bruce Semmons featuring in the results. In the east, the London & Southend Aces organized grass-track events at Laindon on the Arterial Road, Southend.

The south-east had the famous Brands Hatch and Layham's Farm circuits, with plenty of clubs holding race meetings, including Rochester, Green Motor-Cycle Club (Shepperton), Barham (Eastry) and Leatherhead (Randalls Park).

Team racing was held in Essex, when the Stambridge Motor-Cycle Club raced against the Corringham Cobras, with the Stambridge side winning 32-20. The venue for this match might raise a few eyebrows for it took place at Rayleigh Speedway, but this is not to be confused with Rayleigh Weir Stadium, for this was an actual grass-track circuit.

At the end of July, two major events were fought out, with the Southern Counties Championship taking place at Layhams Farm and the Worcestershire Championship being held at Crown Meadow, Evesham. 5,000 spectators turned out to watch the Southern Counties Championship and it wasn't just the south-east aces who took part, for joining the all-star line-up were Midlanders Dick Tolley and Andy Mackay. Although Mackay, mounted on his OK Supreme machines, took the runners-up position in the 250cc Class and third place in the 650cc Newcomers event, it wasn't Tolley's day, as he suffered from numerous mechanical problems. First place in the Newcomers Class went to Les Graham, while John Humphries had to settle for second spot.

Following some exciting heats, sixteen riders came to the line for the main Championship final, racing for the Matchless Cup over twenty laps of the course. After three laps, it was Les Graham (OK Supreme) who took the lead, soon pulling away from Les Schweiso, John Humphries and Eric Oliver. Later in the race, Schweiso went out with an engine failure, leaving Graham to win the Championship in style from Oliver (Norton), with H. Addie (Rudge) finishing third and W. Merritt (Velo) fourth.

Eric Oliver had the consolation of taking two sidecar victories, with Jack Surtees finishing as runner-up on both occasions. Wally Lock (AJS) also did the double, winning the 350cc and 650cc finals, both in a speed of 47.68mph, which was a track record at the time.

In the Midlands area, the Evesham Motor Club organized the annual Worcestershire Championship at Crown Meadow, although they were also running events at Fish Inn Meadow, Broadway. Wilmot Evans took victory in both the 250cc and 350cc finals on his Triumph, while C. Stanley won the Novice final and Tommy Westwood, along with passenger Bill Evans, had a victorious sidecar double, but all eyes were on the big 500cc Solo Classes. In the Unlimited final, Bob Foster and Roger Wise had a wheel-to-wheel battle. Earlier in the day, Foster had already beaten Wise by a fraction in their heat, but in the final, it was Wise who passed the Cheltenham rider on the last bend to snatch victory.

So for the showdown, and the 1939 Worcestershire Championship final was certainly that, as Foster and Wise swapped places throughout the twenty laps. On the fifteenth lap, Wise started to get some clutch problems and this allowed Foster to pull away and win by about three yards. Foster's winning time for the twenty laps was 9min 34.6sec, with Richie Reynolds coming through to finish third.

While mentioning the Midlands area, there was a series of meetings that took place at a very famous place, namely Alton Towers in Staffordshire. The East Midland ACU held meetings on a monthly basis on a 1066-yard mountain-type circuit. Top riders who rode at the venue included Freddie Hudson, Dick Tolley, Andy Mackay and George Milton, with the latter winning the Tower Trophy in May of this year.

Another major event during 1939 was the Brands Hatch Championship, which saw Wally Lock defeat an all-star line-up that included Les Schwieso, Pete Lansdale, Eric Oliver and Bill Hallett, when winning all three solo titles (250cc, 350cc and 650cc). Meanwhile, Jack Surtees won the Sidecar title, after defeating Eric Oliver in a gripping event.

Team events were still popular in 1939, and a selection of the season's results are as follows: Lilleshall 13 Rushmere 11; Taunton 71 Holbeach 36; Blackmore Vale 19 Farleigh Castle 17; Blackmore Vale 23 Farleigh Castle 13; Swindon Works 16 Blackmore Vale 20; Blackmore Vale 22 Brands Hatch 14; Brands Hatch 148 Cannfield 194.

Although people often think that British riders racing on the continent was a post-1950s activity, the reality was that in 1939, midlanders Wilmot Evans and Oliver Bevan actually raced in an autumn event at Bargliring Meckleburg in Germany.

Sadly, the next few years saw the demise of grass-track racing, as the war effort took over.

1939 Roll Of Honour

All England Championships (Farleigh Castle)
350cc – Roger Wise
500cc – Mike Erskine
Individual – Vic Worlock
Sidecar – Eric Oliver

Swainswick Grand Prix
Colin Mead

Southern Centre Championships
350cc – Jack Leonard
Individual – Bert Jones
Novice – A. Holton
Sidecar – Tommy Bounds
Club – Blackmore Vale & Ringwood (Tied)

Worcestershire Championship
Bob Foster

South-Eastern Centre Championships
Solo – Wally Lock
500cc Sidecar – G.R. Crowe
560cc Sidecar – Eric Oliver

Brands Hatch Championships
250cc, 350cc and 650cc – Wally Lock
Sidecar – Jack Surtees

Sittingbourne Grand Prix
Jack Colver

Moseley Grand Prix
Jack Sneyd

Ramsgate Cinque Ports Trophy
Pete Lansdale

Uttoxeter Cup Final
Doug Perks

Southern Counties Championship
& 100 Guineas Matchless Trophy (Layham's Farm)
Les Graham

Tim Robbins Challenge Cup (Evesham)
Wilmot Evans

14
GRASS-TRACK RACING
THE WAR YEARS

The vast majority of grass-track racing closed down during the war years, from September 1939 until the end of 1945. In the Wessex Centre, West Wilts Motor Club cancelled their scheduled meeting at Farleigh Castle in September '39, but they did, however, organize a meeting in May 1940. The wartime meeting was attended by 4,000 spectators, who witnessed top riders Roger Wise, Colin Mead, Vic Worlock, Stan Lanfear and Wilf Sleightholme clean up for the final time until 1946.

During 1942-43, three meetings were staged at Chard, Somerset in aid of the town's 'Holidays at Home Fund'. Grass-track racing was also held at Worcester in 1943. More clubs started to hold race meetings in 1944 though, mostly in aid of the war effort, and these included the West Bristol Club at Filton, Dursley, Pontypool in Wales, and the Spa ground in Gloucester. Meetings were also staged at Derby, Leicester, Grimsby, Hereford, Rochester and Chatham, but all of these were very much charitable fundraising events.

One of these meetings took place in aid of the Red Cross and was organized by the Coventry Motor Cycle Racing Club. The title in the programme promises 'This is the finest entry of any grass speedway meeting ever promoted in Great Britain', with the list of competitors for the 18 September event certainly reading like a who's who of racing. Included were: Fred Tuck, Vic Pitcher, Don Houghton, Jim Cashmore, Alex Gray, Lou Lawson, Bill Hopkins and Roger Wise, while the non-starters included international stars Jack Parker, Bob Foster and Monty Banks. The results of the finals were:

350cc final – First: Ron Carvill (OK Supreme), Second: A.R. Ellison (Triumph), Third: H.A. Nash (BSA)
500cc final – First: Ron Clarke (Speedway Jap), Second: Eric Chitty (Speedway Jap), Third: Reg Lambourne (Velo)
Unlimited final – First: Ron Clarke (Speedway Jap), Second: Vic Worlock (Speedway Jap), Third: E. Appleby (Jap)
Red Cross Trophy (for the 12 fastest riders) – First: Ron Clarke (Speedway Jap), Second: Vic Worlock (Speedway Jap), Third: Bill Hopkins (Martin Jap).

There was a big speedway connection at the meeting, with both Eric Chitty and Ron Clarke using their speedway engines. Chitty was a top Canadian speedway rider who rode with West Ham, while Ron Clarke was an ace rider at New Cross.

Official Programme   **Price 3d.**

The Hawks Motor Club
MOTOR-CYCLE
GRASS-TRACK
RACING

Saturday, August 19th, 1944

AT THE

RACECOURSE GRASS TRACK, EVESHAM ROAD.

First Event **2** p.m. prompt

Alcohol Fuel only is used.   Petrol strictly Barred.

RUN UNDER A.C.U. RULES AND A.C.U. PERMIT

Signals :- **Red** - *Stop,*   **Green** - *Start,*
Yellow - *Last Lap,*   **Check** - *Finish.*

All Races of Four Laps with Clutch-Starts.

OFFICIALS—
Judge : A. WILLIAMS, Esq.,
Gatekeepers: H. H. BLISS, Esq. F. CHESHIRE, Esq. C. G. PRIOR Esq,
Steward of Meeting :   LEN. BLISS, Esq
Chief Timekeeper : S. BLOXSOME, Esq.
Competitors Marshall : T. LAILEY, Esq.
Pit Stewards : W. HILLS, Esq., L. SMITH, Esq.
Public Equipment: MAX YOUNG, Esq.
Track Steward: P. R. SMITH, Esq.   Prize Steward: C. MARSH, Esq,

Medical and First Aid : St. John Ambulance Brigade
and British Red Cross Society.

GROVE, WELLINGTON PRESS, CHELTENHAM

Hawks programme, 1944.

MOTOR CYCLE
GRASS TRACK RACING

AT

FILTON SPEEDWAY

Promoted by West Bristol Motor Cycle and Car Club

Whit-Monday, 29th May, 1944

at 2.30 p.m.

A.C.U. Permit M.20

OFFICIALS

A.C.U. Steward ..	.. ...ING, Esq.
Club Stewards	.. {W. H. SEARLE, Esq. / J. BRYMER, Esq.
Clerk of the Course ..	.. W. O. WATKINS, Esq.
Judge and Timekeeper	.. V. C. ANSTICE, Esq.
Starter	.. A. W. MORRISH, Esq.
Machine Examiner ..	.. D. HARRISON, Esq.
Secretary and Organiser	.. E. H. STANBURY, Esq.

PROCEEDS IN AID OF BRISTOL'S OWN FUND

Our thanks to J. WINDELL, Esq. for the use of the track

Fuel containing NO PETROL is being used

MOTOR RACING IS DANGEROUS

The promoters do not hold themselves responsible
for any accidents

A further meeting will be announced in the press

OFFICIAL PROGRAMME SIXPENCE

Mason & Sons, Printers, Brist

Filton programme, 1944.

The War Years Roll Of Honour (1944)

Pontypool Championships
350cc and 500cc – Reg Lambourne

West Bristol Championships
350cc – Tommy Wood
Searle Trophy – Broncho Slade
Unlimited – Freddie Brown

Gloucester Grand Prix
Vic Worlock

Red Cross Trophy (Coventry)
Ron Clarke

15
GRASS-TRACK RACING
1945

With the end of wartime hostilities, a boom period began for grass-track racing, with large crowds reported all over Great Britain. There was still no official National or British Championships, but there were plenty of highlights and events to record.

Down at Bristol, the Bristol Aeroplane Company joined forces with the West Bristol Motor-Cycle and Car Club to hold a meeting at B.A.C.'s Sports Ground in Patchway on Monday 21 May. A large holiday crowd was in attendance, with the results as follows:

350cc final – First: K.J. Powell, Second: Pat Waterman, Third: G.E. Bowen
500cc final – First: Pat Waterman, Second: R. Moore, Third: E.W. Trappitt
Unlimited final – First: Roger Wise, Second: Pat Waterman, Third: G.E. Bowen
Six Fastest final – First: Pat Waterman, Second: Roger Wise, Third: C.A. Dickens

Despite the fact that Pat Waterman and Roger Wise took the main final wins, it was Bill Hopkins who circumnavigated the course in the fastest time of the day, clocking 1min 33.8sec in heat four of the 350cc Class.

Gloucestershire certainly came to the fore with some excellent racing, and one such event was held by the Cotswold Motor Club at Sudmeadow Road, Hempsted, with the winners being Reg Lambourne (350cc), Vic Worlock (500cc), F. Brown (Unlimited), Lou Lawson (Six Fastest final) and Bill Hopkins (Match Race).

Another meeting was the Littledean Grass-track Championship, which was staged in aid of the 'Littledean Welcome Home Fund'. It was the first meeting to be held in the Forest of Dean at Cinderford. The track measured 350 yards and over 1,000 people saw Bruce Semmens sweep to victory ahead of Jim Cashmore and Stan Rea.

The Cotswold Motor Club ran another meeting at Overton Farm, Cranham, near Stroud in aid of the 'Cranham Welcome Home Fund'. The Cranham circuit measured 350 yards and in what was a full programme of thirty-six races, the results were:

250cc final – First: Fred Lloyd, Second: Bill Davies, Third: Fred Smith
350cc final – First: Colin Mead, Second: Jim Cashmore, Third: Stan Rea
Clubmans final – First: Bill Hopkins, Second: Stan Rea, Third: A. Gregory
Match Race – First: Colin Mead, Second: Bill Hopkins, Third: Stan Rea
Cranham Challenge Cup – First: Lou Lawson, Second: Colin Mead, Third: Jim Cashmore
Open – First: H.E. Caunt, Second: Jim Cashmore, Third: Colin Mead
Standard Machine final – First: Colin Mead, Second: Fred Lloyd, Third: C. Langston
Six Fastest final – First: Lou Lawson, Second: Jim Cashmore, Third: H.E. Gaunt

OFFICIAL PROGRAMME : SIXPENCE

CHELTENHAM MOTOR CLUB

GRASS TRACK RACING

STATION FIELD, EVESHAM ROAD
(OPPOSITE RACECOURSE)

SEPTEMBER 1st, 1945

First Race : 3 o'clock.

Held under the General Competition Rules and Supplementary Regulations of the A.C.U., Western Centre.

Permit No. L291

OFFICIALS :

A.C.U. Steward : Mr. H. P. BAUGHAN.

Stewards for the Meeting :
Messrs. G. H. GOODALL, J. ASHMEAD, C. LOCKE.

Judge : Mr. A. A. WILLIAMS.

Treasurer : Mr. V. BULLOCK.

Secretary of the Meeting and Clerk of the Course :
J. H. HEATHFIELD,
6 CLARENCE PARADE, CHELTENHAM.

Cheltenham programme, 1945.

PROGRAMME   **6d.**

GRASS TRACK
MOTOR CYCLE RACING
MEETING

(Held under the General Competition Rules of the A.C.U.). Permit No. F.110.

AT

WHITLEY AERODROME,

By kind permission of the Management (Messrs. SIR W. G. ARMSTRONG-WHITWORTH
AIRCRAFT, Ltd.)

SUNDAY, SEPTEMBER 16th, 1945,

COMMENCING AT 2-30 P.M.

Proceeds to Coventry and Warwickshire Hospital

OFFICIALS:

Clerk of the Course	CYRIL LORD
Chief Club Steward and Commentator	VERNON MUSLIN
Assistant Club Steward	W. A. FANNON
Pit Steward	F. ESHELBY
Time Keepers	A. SAWARD, A. BROMWICH
Starter	N. C. DIXON
Machine Examiner	P. WHEELER
Chief Marshal	H. TILLEY
A.C.U. Steward	F. S. SMITH
Programmes	Mrs. J. JORDAN and Ladies of the Club
Treasurer	G. H. BLAIR, A.F.C.
Secretary of Meeting	KEITH MOULTON, 62, Broadway, Coventry

---

PARBURY BROS. LTD., GROVE STREET, COVENTRY.

Whitley programme, 1945.

Racing gets underway at Gloucester Spa.

Finally, for the crowd of some 2,000 spectators, there was also a team event featuring Cotswold Motor-Cycle Club *v.* West Bristol Motor-Cycle and Light Car Club, which ended in a 3-3 draw.

On 16 September, the Antelope Motor-Cycle Club of Coventry organized a meeting at Whitley Aerodrome. The competitors for this event included some very famous names in the world of motorcycling, namely Bill Boddice and Bob Foster (road racing), Sam Seston (trials) plus Jock Grierson and Billy Hole (speedway). Also competing was Jimmy Alves, who became the first-ever British Trials 'Star' Champion in 1950, and a Triumph works rider, Bob Foster, was the star of the meeting, taking victory in the 600cc, Grand Prix and Fastest Six events. Meanwhile, Ron Carvill took victory in the 250cc Class, and Jimmy Alves won the 350cc event.

A meeting was held at Bream in the Forest of Dean on 13 October, when Worcester's Reg Lambourne had a field day, with no less than four final victories in the 350cc, 500cc, Unlimited and Six Fastest events. Tewkesbury's Colin Mead collected three second places, while Bill Hopkins from Didmarton won the Clubmans final, with Pat Waterman emerging victorious from the Match Race final.

Hereford Racecourse events certainly pulled in the top riders, as a meeting staged on 22 September indicated. Organized by the Hereford Sports Motor-Cycle Club, the field included Reg Lambourne, Pat Waterman, Colin Mead, Lou Lawson, Ben Collins, Stan Rea, Les Beaumont, Jim Cashmore, Len Bayliss, Frank Evans, Bill Hopkins, Mike Erskine, Bruce Semmens, Vic Worlock and local rider Ray Harris, on a 500cc Douglas.

Official Programme.   Price Sixpence.

Cranham Welcome Home Fund

(Registered War Charity).

The Cotswold Motor Cycle Club

Speedway Racing

OVERTOWN FARM

(By kind permission of W. A. CLOSE, ESQ.)

Saturday, October 6th,
at 2.30 p.m.

Held under A.C.U. Rules and A.C.U. Permit No. L296.

OFFICIALS.

A.C.U. Steward : Mr. J. Heathfield.   Judge : Dr. G. A. Hoffman.

Starter : W/O. Buffington.   Treasurer of the Meeting : Mr. W. Merrett.

Programme Director : Mrs. S. M. Williams. Prize Steward : Mr. M. Morris.

Public Marshall : P. C. Handley (Glos. Const.)

Competitors Marshall : Mr. E. Groves.

Timekeepers :

Mr. F. N. Schobel.   Mr. G. Heggie.   Mr. L. Chiswell.

Statistics : Mr. J. S. Ashmead.   Mr. D. E. Lewis.

Pit Stewards : Mr. S. Walls. Mr. G. Thomas. Mr. S. Smith.

Track Stewards :

Mr. J. Clayton. Mr. L. Whaite. Mr. G. Scott. Mr. G. H. Gittings.

Medical Officer in Attendance :

Dr. Wilson-Carey.   Dr. C. U. Aitchison, M.R.C.S., L.R.C.P.

Public Announcement Equipment : Messrs. Archie Smith, Glos.

First Aid : Members British Red Cross, Stroud 19 Div.

Organised by the Cotswold Motor Club.

Competition Secretary : D. E. Lewis.

Hon. Organising Secretary : J. S. Ashmead, 27, Kendal Rd., Longlevens.

Cranham Welcome Home Fund.

Chairman : Rev. Thomas, The Rectory, Cranham.

Sports Secretary : E. J. Brown, The Paddock, Cranham.

PUBLIC NOTICE.

This track is well roped for your safety—keep outside the ropes ! The Organisers, or their Officials, cannot accept any liability for injury, loss or damage to person or property.

Cranham programme, 1945.

The programme for the meeting included a profile of Welsh rider Roy Zeal, which revealed that he was also a goalkeeper for Newport County FC, as well as a professional comedian!

In Huntingdonshire, grass-track racing also took place at the Eastfield Speed Track, situated in Eastfield Road, Peterborough.

The War Years Roll Of Honour (1945)

Pathfinders Littleover Championship (Derby)
Tommy Bateman

West Bristol Championships
350cc – Freddie Brown
500cc – Lou Lawson

South-Western Championship
Fred Tuck

King's Norton Grand Prix
Reg Lambourne

Antelope Grand Prix (Coventry)
Bob Foster

Kinver Grand Prix
Oliver Bevan

Littledean Championship
Bruce Semmens

Cranham Challenge Cup
Lou Lawson

16
GRASS-TRACK RACING
1946

With the war over, 1946 was the start of an era that could aptly be described at the golden age of grass-track, with massive crowds turning out to see all-star line-ups all over Britain.

Farleigh Castle opened up again in April, with a new track and a new trophy – the Farleigh Castle Plate – which was subsequently awarded at each meeting to the rider recording the fastest time of the day. The first winner of the new trophy was Roger Wise, while a new name that appeared in the programme was that of Lew Coffin, who was, of course, destined to become a real grass-track great.

The year saw meetings at Farleigh Castle raced in front of crowds of up to 8,000, and to celebrate the upsurge in support, the West Wilts Motor Club brought out a special souvenir picture album. Several star riders won events at Farleigh Castle during the year, and these included Roger Wise, Wilf Sleightholme, Pat Waterman, Vic Worlock, Graham Parry, Charlie Hayden and Alan Chambers. While sidecars were a bit thin on the ground, the driver to beat was Carterton's John Browne, who also took the year's Wessex Centre title. Other sidecar winners at Farleigh Castle included Tommy Bounds and Jack Surtees. The Centre Championships were held at the Wiltshire venue, with the Solo Champions being Jack Leonard (350cc) and Stan Lanfear (500cc). Among other notable achievements during the year, Vic Worlock set the track record at Farleigh Castle by clocking 1min 50.2sec on 12 May.

Large numbers of spectators were also flocking to other venues in the Wessex area, including the clubs at Highworth, Bath & West, North Wilts, Frome, Bristol Combined, West Bristol, Shepton Mallett and the Douglas MCC. The latter organized a June meeting at Parkwall Farm, Longwell Green in Bristol. The event was connected with Hanham Folk Centre and the riders present included Dick Bradley, Dick Wyatt, Stan Lanfear, Billy Hole and Graham Parry.

The Highworth club organized meetings at Mr Case's Farm, South Marston, near Swindon, with the Wise brothers (Reg, Ken and Roger) taking an active part in the organizing committee, as well as Roger winning several of the finals. The Bristol Motor-Cycle Club was also active, and ran a meeting at the Brickworks Field in Hambrook.

In Cornwall, racing took place at the foot of the china clay hills near St Austell at Treviscoe. Using a field given by J. Bazley, the venue was known as Treviscoe Speedway and top riders at the venue included Ivan Kessell, Ken Slee, Ben Slee, Des Tamblyn, Cecil Macey, Bob Collins and a youngster called Adrian Kessell. Team racing was also staged at Treviscoe and matches included Cornwall v. Gloucester and Devon/Cornwall v. Bournemouth/Dorset. The Bournemouth/Dorset team was a real powerhouse unit and consisted of Charlie Hayden, Dink Philpotts, Alan Chambers, Herby Hayden and Tommy Crutcher.

GRASS TRACK & SPEEDWAY September 14, 1946

GRASS TRACK *and* SPEEDWAY

| Vol. 1 No 5 | SEPTEMBER 14, 1946 | On Sale Fortnightly | THREEPENCE |

Doug Perks stages a Come-back

Exclusive to Grass Track and Speedway.

DOUG RIDING BACK TO STARDOM

Grasstrack and Speedway *magazine, 14 September 1946.*

Brands Hatch programme, 1946.

John Browne and Jim Smith.

Staying in Cornwall, the Pendennis Motor-Cycle and Light Car Club organized meetings at the Recreation Ground in Falmouth. President of the club was Lord Sempill and, in 1946, the Cornwall clubs were affiliated to the South-Western Centre. During the race intervals, extra entertainment was provided for the spectators and this included surf board racing, trick riding, a chariot race and midget car demonstrations.

The St Austell Motor Club, which organized racing at Rocky Park prior to the war, came back with two new venues at Pennans, Grampound and Mr Inch's Showfield, Duporth. It was interesting to note that the Hampshire & Dorset riders came down to Cornwall on a regular basis, and as well as the riders previously mentioned, they also included Bingley Cree and Cyril Quick.

Rather like the Farleigh Castle Plate in the Wessex Centre, a J.W. Higman Helmet was won at each meeting that the St Austell club hosted. They also organized extra entertainment, including Harry Skirrow – a one-armed midget-car racer! Over the border in Devon, the West of England Motor Club held meetings at Great Chalk, Bishopsteignton.

Further up country in the Western Centre, the Cotswold Motor-Cycle Club certainly organized a lot of meetings on many different circuits around Gloucestershire and over the border in Herefordshire. Some of their venues included Coalway, Tibberton, Coberley, Littledean, Hempsted (Gloucester), Staunton, Bream, Ledbury and Staverton (on the RAF airfield). All the meetings were charitable fundraising activities and included a series of Grand Prix events. Crowd figures varied from 1,000 to 4,000 for the racing, which was sometimes on oval tracks as small as 350 yards in length. Top riders at these meetings included Bill Hopkins, Bruce Semmens, Lou Lawson, Jim Cashmore and Reg Lambourne, with Semmens being triumphant in two of the Grand Prix events. Worcester's Reg Lambourne took the Gloucestershire Championship at the Spa Ground, mounted on a Jap, with Ray Beaumont (AJS) finishing as runner-up, while Les Beaumont (Matchless Jap) was third.

Going up to the Midlands, it was the same story, with success after success. At a Birmingham Motor-Cycle Club meeting in April at Mappleborough, it was the Wessex Centre rider Roger Wise that took the honours, winning both the Invitation and Unlimited finals. Roger also went on to break the track record when he defeated Cheltenham's Bob Foster to win the Eight Fastest Riders final and collect the Golden Wing helmet. Third place, incidentally, went to Jim Tolley, grandfather of Ryan Tolley,

Adrian Kessell, going through his paces.

John Browne and Jim Smith in action.

The start of a race at Hanham.

who was the winner of the year 2000 British Under-21 Grass-track Championship.

Roger Wise was a regular in the Midlands and he featured in another battle that took place at the War Memorial Park on Kenilworth Road in Coventry. The event, organized by the Coventry & Warwickshire Motor Club, saw Tewkesbury's Colin Mead as Roger's opponent. In the 350cc final, it was Roger who won on the last lap, while in the Unlimited final, the result was reversed following a great scrap.

The famous name in the south-east was Brands Hatch and, during 1946, crowds of 10,000 were reported and it was also the year that a team from Northern Ireland visited the Kent circuit. A team representing Brands Hatch took on a side from the Antelope club at Whitley Aerodrome in Warwickshire, and it was the Midlanders that came out on top with a 24-12 victory. This was something of a surprise when you look at the Brands Hatch team, which consisted of Ted Kempson, Wally Lock, Harry Ditchburn, Eric Oliver and Les Schweiso. Eric Oliver also partook in both the Solo and Sidecar events at the meeting, winning both sidecar finals. On his way to glory, Eric defeated another driver destined for road racing fame, namely Bill Boddice. Andy Mackay was the solo star of the day, winning the 350cc, Unlimited and Antelope Championship finals. In the latter, Len Bayliss was runner-up, while Dick Tolley finished third.

Other highlights in the Midlands during the year included Dick Tolley breaking Freddie Hudson's track record at Chaddesley Corbett in Worcestershire. 2,500 spectators watched Worcester's Reg Lambourne win the 500cc, Unlimited and Five Fastest

South Marston programme.

finals at Hopcrofts Holt, Banbury in North Oxfordshire. At West Bromwich, Doug Perks enjoyed the deep mud to take victory in no less than four finals. The Shropshire Championships were staged at Bayston Hill, with Dick Tolley emerging as the main winner.

In the East Midlands, 10,000 spectators were in attendance at the Wingfield Park Championships on 24 September. Organized by Pathfinders (Derby) Motor-Cycle Club, the event was run on a mountain-style grass-track circuit. The large crowd saw Eric Oliver (Norton) defeat Bill Boddice (Ariel) and J.S. Jenkins (Ariel) to win the Sidecar Championship, while Len Bayliss (Triumph) took the Solo title

OFFICIAL PROGRAMME — SIXPENCE
HIGHWORTH M.C. & L.C. CLUB
GRASS TRACK RACES
(Open to Wessex Centre A.C.U.)
Held under Permit No. 77 and subject to the
General Competition Rules of the Auto Cycle Union
at
Mr. CASE'S FARM, SOUTH MARSTON, Nr. SWINDON
on
SUNDAY, SEPTEMBER 22nd, 1946
First Race, 2.30 p.m.
OFFICIALS
Stewards:
C. H. KING, Esq. (appointed by the Wessex Centre A.C.U.),
T. MITCHELL, Esq. (appointed by the Organising Club)
Judge Timekeeper: V. ANSTICE, Esq. (A.C.U.)
Starters: S. SMITH, Esq., A. PORTER, Esq.
Lap Scorer: M. OWEN, Esq.
Machine Examiner: H. JARMAN, Esq.
Paddock Marshals:
K. K. WISE, Esq., J. TYLDESLEY, Esq., and A. N. NELMES, Esq.
Racing Commentator: REG. WISE, Esq.
Track Supervisor: H. TREMBLIN, Esq.
Organising Committee:
REG. F. J. WISE (Chairman), S. R. WISE (Captain), H. JARMAN,
S. SMITH, K. K. WISE (Treasurer), T. E. MITCHELL,
P. DELL (Secretary)
Clerk of the Course and Secretary of Meeting:
P. DELL, 1, SWINDON STREET, HIGHWORTH, WILTS.
Parking Marshals: SWINDON & DISTRICT M.C.

The Red Cross Ambulance (Wilts 19 & 21) is in attendance by kind permission of the Officers Commanding.
Prior to the start of each event the names of riders competing will be announced and the results and times will be given after each race.

from runner-up Alf Briggs (Triumph) and third-placed Eric Oliver (Jap).

The Midlands-based *Grass-track and Speedway* magazine of the era held a Most Popular Rider of the Year award, with the result being: First: Dick Tolley, Equal Second: Roger Wise and Andy Mackay, Fourth: Oliver Bevan.

During the year, meetings in the Midlands area were held at Marden (Coventry & Warks), Leek Wotton (Coventry & Warks), Astwood Bank (Redditch), Chaddesley Corbett, Bayston Hill, Romsley (West Bromwich), Warstock (King's Norton), Mappleborough Green, Rushmere and Crown Meadow. In fact, it was at Crown Meadow (Evesham), that the prestigious Worcestershire Championship took place, with the result being: First: Dick Tolley, Second: Len Bayliss, Third: C. Willmott, Fourth: Colin Mead.

The north west of England also dished up some exciting action, with two Cheshire clubs holding meetings at Winsford and Chester. The major star in this area was Andy Mackay. Meanwhile, in the south, Andover Motor-Cycle and Light Car Club was formed, with the top club member being sidecar ace Tommy Bounds. At their first meeting, however, it was thirty-seven-year-old Reg Higham who took the Novice award.

Bonny Good from Devizes began his racing career mounted on a 500cc Wallis Jap in 1946, and became a member of the Blackmore Vale club. Bonny enjoyed his initial year of racing and the highlight was when he clocked the fastest time at the Cannfield circuit. While on the subject of the Blackmore Vale club, famed Rudge rider Gerald Selby was the team captain during this year.

Farleigh Castle programme, 1946.

BANBURY AUTO CLUB

Affiliated to South Midland Central A.C.U.
Permit No. N.19.

❖❖❖❖❖❖❖❖❖❖❖❖❖❖❖❖❖❖❖❖❖❖❖❖❖❖❖❖❖❖❖❖❖❖

Motor-Cycle Grass Track ... Speedway ...

❖❖❖❖❖❖❖❖❖❖❖❖❖❖❖❖❖❖❖❖❖❖❖❖❖❖❖❖❖❖❖❖❖❖

MIDDLETON ROAD, BANBURY

(By kind permission of Mr. W. Stroud)

On Sunday, April 28th, 1946

Official Opening at 2 p.m.

OFFICIALS:

Medical Officer: Dr. C. GARDINER-HILL

Judge: F. E. LAMPITT

A.C.U. Steward: T. SHEPHEARD.   Records: H. C. LAPTHORNE.

Clerk of Course: R. E. CRANSTONE.

Announcer: W. H. RUSSELL.

Timekeepers: A. WILLIS and D. HUNT.

Starter: E. THORNETT.   Scrutineer: H. A. OWEN.

Paddock Marshalls: E. BURTON and H. O. OWEN.

Hon. Secretaries of the Meeting and Club:

L. G. POULSON,   E. BURTON,
15, High Street, Banbury.   46, Causeway, Banbury.

Hon. Treasurer: R. L. PASCALL, c/o 15, High Street, Banbury.

Public Address Equipment (A. A. Boote) by Banbury Ciné Sound.

Members of St. John Ambulance Brigade in attendance.

WARNING. Motor Racing is Dangerous. — You are present at this Meeting entirely at your own risk, and the ticket of admission is issued subject to the condition that all persons having any connection with the promotion and/or organisation and/or conduct of the Meeting, including the owners of the land and drivers and owners of the vehicles and passengers on the vehicles, are absolved from all liability in respect of personal injury (whether fatal or otherwise) to you or damage to your property howsoever caused. **The track is well roped for your own safety. Keep outside the rope.**

NO BETTING ALLOWED

Banbury programme, 1946.

OFFICIAL PROGRAMME   -   -   -   PRICE SIXPENCE

EVESHAM MOTOR CYCLE CLUB
(Midland Centre A.C.U.)

President   -   -   Rupert De la Bere Esq., M.P.

WORCESTERSHIRE CHAMPIONSHIP
GRASS TRACK RACES

Crown Meadow, Evesham
Monday, August 5th, 1946

Stewards of the Meeting: Mr. F. S. Smith (A.C.U.), Dr. S. Goodwin, Mr. A. R. Mansell and Mr. Tim Robbins (Club).

Judge: Timekeeper (A.C.U.):   Machine Examiners:
Mr. S. Robinson.   Mr. A. Taylor.   Mr. J. Sinclair and Mr. P. K. Sollis.

Paddock Marshalls: Mr. D. Holmes and Mr. H. C. Young.

Track Marshalls: Evesham and Broadway Club Members.

Medical Attendants: Evesham Division St. Johns Ambulance Brigade.

Clerk of the Course and Secretary of the Meeting: Mr. H. J. Griffiths.

Treasurer: Mr. O. Edwards.   Public Address System: Messrs. Spencers, Redditch.

COMPETITORS AND THEIR MACHINES

O. Bevan	350 D.M.V.	G. Little	350 Velocette	G. Griffin	500 J.A.P.
S. G. Harris	250 O.K.	G. L. Brown	350 A.J.S.	T. H. Westwood	500 T.H.W.
R. Pointer	350 Triumph	L. Fulham	350 A.J.S.	W. Evans	500 G.H.C.
Les Mills	350 Mills-Jap	W. L. Dawson	350 D.M.W.	D. Sheen	350 Excelsior
S. T. Seston	350 J.A.P.	T. Swallow	350 O.K.	C. Mead	350 Mead Sp.
J. MacPhail	350 A.J.S.	W. Phillips	350 A.J.S.	N. Aston	230 Velocette
E. W. Commander	250 Triudge	J. H. Swallow	350 Rudge	L. Beaumont	350 J.A.P.
C. Willmott	350 Triumph	F. T. Buckle	250 Velocette	R. Beaumont	350 A.J.S.
L. J. Bayliss	350 Triumph	C. Green	350 New Imp	R. T. Pritchard	350 New Imp
J. Williams	350 Norton	G. A. Hodges	350 O.K.	J. Bosworth	350 Triumph
V. Holcroft	350 A.J.S.	R. Tolley	500 Ariel	G. H. Cole	500 G.H.C.
W. A. Phillips	500 J.A.P.	A. Lidgate	500 Triumph	J. Tolley	350 Velocette
Roger Wise	250 Enfield	J. Lidgate	350 Velocette	R. Reynolds	350 New Imp
T. Gyselnyck	350 Velocette	P. Harris	500 J.A.P.	R. D. Winwood	350 New Imp
W. H. Longford	500 A.S.P.	W. B. Stanford	348 Rudge	T. Deadman	500 T.D.S.

FLAGS

Union Jack—Start.   Red—Stop.   Yellow—Last Lap.
Green—Road Clear.   Black Flag with Number—Motor Cycle bearing that Number Stop Immediately.   Chequered—Finish.

Crown Meadow programme, 1946.

The Bournemouth Motor Club held racing at Tolpuddle, while down the road at Hamble, the Southampton club ran events. Southampton's skipper was Bert Morris, but it was twenty-six-year-old Jimmy Squibb who caught the eye. Jimmy, who was destined for a long speedway career, represented the Southampton grass-track team, riding Jap and Matchless machines.

The Yeo Vale club was formed in the South-Western Centre during the year, and club member Lew Coffin started on his route to success with a 350cc win at Bristol. Racing was also strong in the Swansea and Port Talbot areas of south Wales, with the Williams brothers and the Treseder brothers being prominent, although it was Pat Waterman who was triumphant in the Neath Open Championship.

Other meetings for 1946 included Folkestone (Sports Ground), Barnsley Motor-Cycle and Light Car Club (Wombwell Greyhound Stadium), Peterborough (Eastfield), Hereford (Racecourse), Moseley (Lowsonford), Brands Hatch Combine, Sittingbourne, Cotswold Motor Club (Gloucester Spa), Wrexham (Bangor-on-Sea), Crewe & South Cheshire (Haslington), Blackmore Vale Motor-Cycle Club (Okeford Hill) and Ashford (Mersham).

Finally, the Warrington & District Motor Club obtained national publicity when they ran three successful semi-mountain-type meetings. The nationwide publicity occurred when the local council of churches protested against Sunday racing. Thankfully, the furore blew over when the Warrington club were able to come to a satisfactory agreement.

1946 Roll Of Honour

Moseley Grand Prix
Jack Sneyd

Neath Open Championship
350cc, 500cc and Open – Pat Waterman
Novice – Llew Hunkin

South-Eastern Championships
250cc – Bill Hallett
350cc – Jock West
650cc – Eric Oliver
Sidecar – Eric Oliver

Worcestershire Championship
Dick Tolley

Wessex Centre Championships
350cc – Jack Leonard
500cc – Stan Lanfear
Sidecar – John Browne
Club – West Bristol

West Of England Championship
Les Beaumont

Brands Hatch Championships
350cc – Wally Lock
500cc – Johnny Lockett
Sidecar – Arthur Horton

Chester & Cheshire Centre Championship
Andy Mackay

Gloucestershire Championship
Reg Lambourne

Autounion Trophy (Rushmere)
Andy Mackay

Ledbury Grand Prix
Bruce Semmens

Staverton Grand Prix
Richie Reynolds

Hereford Challenge Trophy
Mike Beddoe

Southampton Championship
Bob Oakley

Staunton Grand Prix
Colin Mead

Highworth Grand Prix
Roger Wise

17
GRASS-TRACK RACING
1947

The *Bristol Evening World* handbook which covered speedway, also included a page on the grass-track scene in the Wessex Centre and summed up the grass-track racing scene in Britain as a whole for 1947: 'The tremendous interest in grass-track racing staged in the West Country broke all previous records. It was the finest year ever in the history of the sport. Attendances increased and racing was brilliant'.

This year's Wessex Championship was held by the Highworth Motor-Cycle and Light Car Club at Kingsdown Farm, Kingsdown, near Swindon. A 600-yard circuit was used, with the board of the Wessex Centre making a particular request for an 's' bend to be included. The big winners at the prestigious event were Stan Lanfear (350cc), Richie Reynolds (Individual) and Don Slate (Sidecar).

The average attendance figures at Kingsdown during 1947 were around the 5,000 mark. However, the public didn't just turn out to watch the regular aces from the Wessex, Southern, Midland and Western Centres, but top-class match races as well, such as Split Waterman *v.* Freddie Williams, Jack Parker *v.* Roger Wise, and George Wilks *v.* Bill Kitchen.

Other venues in the Wessex area included Shepton Mallet, Farleigh Castle, Frome and the Bath & West Clubs. In the south-east, meanwhile, Brands Hatch played host to the stars and drew crowds in the region of 13,000. Towards the end of the season, history was made on 4 September, when BBC cameras visited the famous circuit to record the first-ever grass-track racing for presentation on television.

However, before then, in the heart of the summer, a very special meeting took place at Brands Hatch on 28 June, when the Brands Hatch Combine organized an unofficial English Championship. It may have been unofficial, but competitors came from far and wide for the All England Star Riders' Championship. Solo entrants included Jack Leonard (Poole), Bert Roger (Chatham), Ted Kempson (Dulwich), Jack Difazio (Frome), Frank Allen (Reading), Roger Wise (Swindon), Andy Mackay (Birkenhead), Len Bayliss (Coventry), Harry Ditchburn (Northfleet), Ron Carvill (Coventry), Wally Lock (Gravesend) and Jack Colver (Plumstead). Sidecar competitors included Stan Appleby (Southampton), Jack Surtees (Forest Hill), Bill Boddice (Birmingham) and Tom Arter (Sevenoaks). There were certainly some very famous names in the world of motor-cycling in that line-up.

The Sidecar final and the 500cc Solo final were broadcast on the BBC light programme, with top motor-cycle commentator of the day Graham Walker (father of Murray) describing the action. Several of the competitors doubled-up and rode in both the Solo and Sidecar Classes, including Eric Oliver, who went on to become a double Champion at the event. Eric, an all-round motorcyclist of course, went on to win the

Fred Smith leads at Cross Hands, Gloucester, in 1947.

Racing at close quarters, as Bonny Good leads Dick Bradley.

World Sidecar Road Racing Championship in the 1950s.

Major results of the All England Championships were as follows:

250cc Lightweight final – First: C.G. Clisby (43.79mph), Second: F. Hayward, Third: Andy Mackay
350cc Junior final – First: Ted Kempson (51.52mph), Second: E. Davis, Third: J. Lockett
650cc Senior final – First: Eric Oliver (52.70mph), Second: Wally Lock, Third: Bert Roger
Sidecar final – First: Eric Oliver (48.84mph), Second: P.A. Seymour, Third: Jack Surtees

Some of the clubs that promoted racing at the one-mile Brands Hatch circuit as part of the Brands Hatch Combine were Owls (Oxted, Westerham, Limpsfield and Sevenoaks), Chatham Motor-Cycle Club, Leatherhead Motor-Cycle Club, Sidcup Motor-Cycle Club and Bermondsey Motor-Cycle Club.

The annual big event in the area was the South-Eastern Centre Championship, which was held on 17 August in hot and dusty conditions. The programme for the event cost 6d and listed some of the solo aces of the day: Jack Difazio, Ted Kempson, Harry Ditchburn, Wally Lock, Alf Bottoms, Bert Roger, Jack Colver and Eric Oliver, with the latter also appearing in the Sidecar event.

Star of speedway, Bert Roger, stormed to victory in the dusty conditions, defeating runner-up R. Frost and third-placed E. Davis to take the Individual Championship in a time of 4min 20.4sec (55.3mph). The other main finals resulted thus:

250cc final – First: F. Hayward (51.69mph), Second: C.G. Clisby, Third: A.H. Joplin
350cc final – First: Eric Oliver (54.92mph), Second: Jack Colver, Third: E. Davis
Sidecars – First: Eric Oliver (50.10mph), Second: Jack Surtees, Third: G. Harris

Another club in the south-east also hit the headlines in 1947, namely Folkestone. At their Folkestone Heights venue, they took on a team from France and defeated them by 26 points to 10. Top English riders at the Kent venue included Don Gray, Bert Roger and W.J. Keel, with the latter winning the Championship race.

Bonny Good had certainly stamped his mark on the grass-track scene in the Southern Centre, winning the Blackmore Vale-staged Reg Stainer Memorial Trophy, the Bournemouth Club's John Philpotts Memorial Trophy, and the Boscombe Championship.

The Bournemouth Club ran meetings at Stalbridge Park and Roke Down, the latter being a 440-yard, smooth oval circuit. The track at Stalbridge Park was also 440 yards in length, but incorporated an 's' bend. Prize money for final wins at the venue varied between £2 and £4. The Bournemouth Club was still closely connected with the Boscombe Carnival and on 13 August, the club organized a meeting in conjunction with this event.

The Blackmore Vale Club was now running at Eastbury Park, Tarrant Gunville, near Blandford, on a track that measured 700 yards and included an 's' bend. To further emphasize the difference in circuits, the Andover Club was staging events at Little Ann Bridge Farm, near Andover, using an 800-yard, smooth, flat track with an 's' bend.

OFFICIAL PROGRAMME

FIRST MEETING   1947 SEASON

Elstree Grass Speedway

WEMBLEY SPEEDWAY SPORTS MOTOR CLUB
Affiliated A.C.U. South Mid. Centre

SUNDAY, 10th AUGUST, 1947

WE INTRODUCE

London Team	v.	Midlands Team
BILL KITCHEN (Wembley)		TIGER HART (Birmingham)
Captain.		Captain.
CYRIL BRINE (Wimbledon)		GEOF. GODWIN (Middlesbro')
SPLIT WATERMAN (Wembley)		PADDY HAMMOND (Norwich)
BILL SALE (Plymouth)		STAN DELL (Birmingham)
ROY CRAIGHEAD (Wembley)		PADDY MILLS (Norwich)
TED MOORE (Exeter)		WILF PLANT (Middlesbrough)

OFFICIALS :

Clerk of the Course	F. LEEKE
Track Manager	G. LUCAS
A.C.U. Steward	To be appointed
Judge and Timekeeper	B. GILBERT
Announcer	ALAN WEBB
Starter	C. LEEKE

St. John Ambulance Brigade will be in attendance.

Programme - - Price 6d.

Elstree programme, 1947.

St. Austell & District Motor Club

(Affiliated to the Cornwall Centre of the A.C.U.)

GRASS

SPEEDWAY

At ROCKY PARK, ST. AUSTELL,

(By kind permission of M. H. Jelbert, Esq.,)

On TUESDAY, AUGUST 26th, 1947, at 6.30 p.m.

Official Programme, Price 6d.

JACK PARKER

This photograph, which we publish by kind permission of the "Speedway Gazette," was taken at Exeter Cinder Track, to which he paid a flying visit whilst staying at St. Austell to compete at our meeting in July last. The badge in his coat lapel is that of St. Austell & District Motor Club, of which he is a member.

Rocky Park programme, 1947.

Meanwhile, the Aston Combine and Bishop's Waltham Clubs used a track at Bishop's Waltham that was 550 yards in circumference, with a slight gradient and decline. To further complicate matters, for solo riders the circuit was oval-shaped, whereas the sidecar competitors had to negotiate an 's' bend.

At Blackmore Vale, they held a collection for Lew Coffin's benefit, and with prize money donated by Ray Scovell and Gerald Selby, a total of over £80 was raised.

Some other interesting points from the Southern Centre included Salisbury's Tony Lewis winning the Novice Speed Championship mounted on a 1929 Sunbeam. Tony, of course, later went on to enjoy a successful speedway career with Poole. Ray Scovell defeated Bingley Cree at the opening of the Ringwood Club's Charlton Marshall track, riding a BSA machine. While on the subject of Ringwood, the club had an attendance of 7,000 people at The Mount in Poulner, to watch Frank Holcombe recording the fastest time of the day.

There were some interesting names appearing on the Southern Centre circuits, and these included Maurice Leonard (father of West Ham, Swindon and Oxford speedway rider Brian), Phil Nex (who was later to taste glory as a top scrambler) and Southampton speedway riders Charlie May, Bert Croucher and Jimmy Squibb.

The Championships, organized by the Bishop's Waltham Club, were held at Aston on 7 September, with the winners being: Dink Philpotts (Individual); T.L. Wood (250cc); Bert Croucher (350cc); A.J. Walker (Intermediate); F. Wheeler (Novice Solo) and R. Robins (Sidecar), with Southampton winning the team shield. There does seem to be some debate over the Individual Champion, however, as some sources suggest that Bert Croucher was triumphant, although filled-in programmes show him as finishing as runner-up to Dink Philpotts.

Down in Cornwall, the St Austell Club started the season with meetings at Duporth, prior to moving back to the popular Rocky Park venue. Speedway aces Jack Parker and Bill Kitchen from Belle Vue and Wembley respectively, came down to race against the top men in the west country, who included the Dorset and Hampshire riders Dink Philpotts, Bingley Cree, the Hayden brothers and Alan Chambers. Local stars included Bob Collins (Probus), Des Tamblyn (Roche) and Adrian Kessell (St Dennis), plus the Hicks brothers, Telfer and Fred, from Carn Brea. Added to this impressive list of competitors were two other speedway riders, namely Broncho Slade and Ivan Kessell. Racing was also held at Bodmin and in South Cornwall, at Kehelland, near Camborne.

In the Midlands, another good season of racing saw some of the early battles taking place on Easter Monday at the Salop Club's venue at Bayston Hill. Sidecar scraps took place between Charlie Winchman (Norton), Bill Boddice (Ariel) and Cecil Smith (Ariel). In the Solo events, a different winner emerged from every class, as follows: Smokey Dawson (350cc); J.L. Davies (Novice); Don Evans (500cc); Dick Tolley (Unlimited) and T. Gyselynck (Handicap).

Another meeting was held on Easter Monday at Wingfield Park, with the winners there being: T.E. Hutchenson (Novice); Freddie Hudson (350cc); A.G. Briggs (500cc); Roger Wise (Underwood Memorial Race), with the Sidecar event being won by J.S. Jenkins.

On Good Friday, the Wrexham Club held an event at The Park in Rossett, which was situated on the main Wrexham to Chester road. The circuit included a double 's' bend and three fast, left-hand bends. On a very cold afternoon, Jack Wilkinson was in fine form, winning both the Standard Machines and 500cc finals, while the other winners were L.A. Bell (Open) and Bob Parker (350cc).

That was just the start of a super season of grass-track action and one of the other items worth mentioning is road racer Cecil Sandford taking victory at the Broadway (Worcester) Motor-Cycle Mountain grass-track. The line-up for this event also featured Ernie Moss, who was the father of 'Days of Glory' supremo Adrian. At the West Midland Grass Racing Group event, the award winners were Dick Tolley (Eric Ratcliffe Memorial Trophy) and Ralph Ellison (Union Auto Club Cup).

The final Wingfield Park meeting of the season had a £291 prize fund, with Len Bayliss winning the Championship title from Peter Orpwood; meanwhile the Sidecar event was won by J.S. Jenkins, ahead of runner-up P.R. Packham. The Underwood Cup, presented to the overall season's best, went to Len Bayliss, while Andy Mackay and Peter Orpwood tied for second position.

At Swadlincote, Burton-on-Trent, racing was staged at Darklands Sports Stadium, where the circuit comprised a large, smooth oval, with a slight incline and long straights. A large crowd witnessed Don Evans, Len Bayliss and Ralph Ellison take part in some fine duels. There were also some female competitors at the meeting, including Molly Briggs and M.J. Davies.

Richie Reynolds collected a double victory at the Prince of Wales track in

Bonny Good receives the Littledean Grand Prix trophy.

Warwickshire, while in the Nantwich Club Championship, it was victory for Ralph Ellison, ahead of Harry Terretta and Bernard Tennent. Based on the three meetings held by the Nantwich Club, the trophies were awarded for the season as follows: Bob Parker (1,000cc); Ralph Ellison (350cc); and Charlie Ford (250cc). Vic Masefield took the award for Local Rider of the Year, while the track record was shared by Bob Parker and Ralph Ellison, who both clocked 2min 1.5sec.

Back at Bayston Hill, Bill Boddice took the Attingham Sidecar Shield, but at the War Memorial Park in Coventry, he had to settle for a share of the honours with Pip Harris. The winner of the Solo Handicap final at this meeting was a very young Cecil Sandford, mounted on a 250cc Velo. Other regulars at the Memorial Park included Ted Commander, Don Evans, Ron Carvill, Wilmot Evans and Eddie Blackwell. 5,000 spectators regularly flocked to this Coventry venue, with the events being held in conjunction with the Coventry Parks Department.

Worcestershire's Freddie Hudson of OK Supreme fame, turned out on a brand new BSA, which gave him a double of second places on its debut at Walsall. At a dusty Bunkers Hill (West Midland Racing Group), Dick Tolley won the Unlimited Championship from T. Groves and Len Bayliss. Meanwhile in Northamptonshire, the Wellingborough Motor Club held a grass-track meeting at the Earls Barton Greyhound Stadium, with Jim Cashmore and Jim Wright sharing the honours. Incidentally, Jim Wright, who also enjoyed a career in speedway with Cradley Heath and Oxford, was sometimes known as Charlie.

The Worcestershire Championship took place at the Old Racecourse at Pershore on 10 August, and it was local rider Reg Lambourne who emerged victorious. Second place in the final went to Dick Tolley, while Ralph Ellison finished third. Lambourne also won both the Unlimited and 500cc finals, with Len Bayliss taking the 350cc final, and Cyril Smith collecting a double Sidecar victory.

The other major event in the Midlands was the Shropshire Championship, which was organized and run by the Salop Club at Bayston Hill. Andy Mackay won both the

Championship and the 500cc finals, while also setting a new track record of 2min 27sec (49mph). Behind Mackay in the Championship final were Len Bayliss (second), Harry Terretta (third) and T. Groves (fourth). Harry Terretta gained some revenge in the 350cc final, finishing ahead of Mackay, while Bill Boddice and Cecil Smith shared the Sidecar victories.

While covering the Midlands, the Leamington Victory Motor-Cycle and Light Car Club ran four meetings at Hiatt's Farm in Ufton. The circuit was situated on the main Leamington to Southam road in Warwickshire. Unlike some venues that have come and gone, the Leamington Club was still holding meetings in the 1980s and 1990s, some fifty years on.

Just to mention one of the meetings at Hiatt's Farm in 1947, Highworth's Roger Wise made a visit on Tuesday 5 August for an evening meeting and came away with victories in the 500cc and Unlimited finals. Jim Cashmore was successful in the 350cc final, while some of the others riders in action that night included Reg Lambourne, Richie Reynolds and Sam Seston.

Having mentioned Bonny Good earlier, it was interesting to note that as well as being a star man in Southern and Wessex Centres, he also did well in the Western Centre. 2,000 spectators witnessed Bonny win no less than three finals at a meeting in the Forest of Dean in Gloucestershire. The event was staged at Greenway Farm, Littledean, and organized by the Popes Hill Club in conjunction with the Gloucester & Cotswold Motor Club. The main final of the meeting saw Bonny triumph in the Littledean Grand Prix, while Richie Reynolds finished second and Swindon's Bob Jones was third. At the end of the meeting, Lady Crawley-Boevey subsequently presented a very proud Bonny with the Grand Prix Cup. Future speedway star Dick Bradley won the Closed to Club and Open finals, while Bill Hopkins did well to finish second in two finals, behind his friend, Bonny.

At the Eastfield Speed Track in Peterborough, team racing was held along speedway lines, with grass straights and dirt on the

Kingsdown programme, 1947.

OFFICIAL PROGRAMME — SIXPENCE

HIGHWORTH M.C. & L.C. CLUB

GRASS TRACK RACES

(Open to Wessex Centre A.C.U.)

Held under Permit No. 117 and subject to the General Competition Rules of the Auto Cycle Union including Racing Regulations Appendix M

at

KINGSDOWN FARM, KINGSDOWN, SWINDON

(by kind permission of Mr. Tom Clare)

on

SUNDAY, 29th JUNE, 1947

First Race 3 p.m.

OFFICIALS

Stewards:

C. H. King, Esq. (appointed by the Wessex Centre A.C.U.)

E. D. Chinn, Esq. (appointed by the Organising Club)

Judge Timekeeper: V. ANSTICE, Esq.

Starters: S. SMITH, Esq.; A. PORTER, Esq.

Lap Scorer: P. DELL, Esq.

Machine Examiner: H. JARMAN, Esq.

Paddock Marshals:

J. TYLDESLEY, Esq., W. G. CUNNINGHAME, Esq., and MEMBERS OF THE HIGHWORTH M.C.C.

Announcer: REG. WISE, Esq.

Track Supervisor: H. TREMBLIN, Esq.

Clerk of the Course: K. K. WISE, Esq.

Secretary of the Meeting:

REG F. J. WISE, Esq., 52, GODDARD AVENUE, SWINDON

Parking Marshals: SWINDON & DISTRICT M.C.C.

The Red Cross Ambulance (Wilts 19 & 21) is in attendance by kind permission of the Officers Commanding

PROCEEDS IN AID OF RED CROSS AMBULANCE FUND

The Swindon Press, Ltd., Swindon.

● Please park your Car at least 6ft. from the Rope

Leamington Victory Motor-Cycle and Light Car Club

*Affiliated to the
Midland Centre
A.C.U.
Permit No. M001*

Grass Track Racing
for Solo Motor-Cycles & Sidecars

at

MR. HIATT'S FARM, UFTON
on Main Leamington-Southam Road

Tuesday, August 5, 1947
Commencing at 6.0 p.m.

OFFICIAL PROGRAMME — SIXPENCE

Ufton programme, 1947.

Official Programme   Price 6d.

Shepton Mallet and District Motor Cycle and Light Car Club

(Affiliated to the A.C.U. Wessex Centre).

This Meeting is organised under Open to Centre Permit No. N. 142 subject to the General Competition Rules of the A.C.U., including Racing Regulations, Appendix M.

Open to Centre

RACE MEETING

Sunday, September 14th, *1947*

First Race 2.30 p.m.

The Mendip Grass Track

Downside, Shepton Mallet

(By kind permission of P. Applegate, Esq.).

OFFICIALS OF THE MEETING :

A.C.U. STEWARD :   CLUB STEWARD :
W. K. RAYMOND, ESQ.   S. SPEED, ESQ.

OFFICIAL TIMEKEEPER, HANDICAPPER & JUDGE :
V. C. ANSTICE, ESQ., A.C.U.

STARTER : MR. S. BARNES.

STARTER'S MARSHALL : S. BEACHAM, ESQ.

MACHINE EXAMINER : C. ENGLAND, ESQ.

PADDOCK MARSHALL : E. COTTLE, ESQ.

ANNOUNCER : D. P. LEAVER, ESQ.

TREASURER OF THE MEETING : H. MEAD, ESQ.

CLERK OF COURSE & SECRETARY OF THE MEETING :
MR. V. O. KEELING, 46, TOWN STREET, SHEPTON MALLET.

MEDICAL OFFICER : DR. R. T. FINN.

First Aid by British Red Cross Society, Somerset 13.

Track : 650 Yards.

FLAGS : UNION JACK—Start. CHEQUERED—Finish. YELLOW—
Last Lap. RED—Race Stop. LIGHT BLUE—Caution.

Spectators are strictly forbidden on the Course.

No Spectators allowed in Competitiors Paddock.

LOUDSPEAKING EQUIPMENT by G. GREGORY, Market Place, Wells.

Catering by the Severn Chair and Marquee Company.

Shepton Mallet programme, 1947.

Farleigh Castle programme, 1947.

bends. A challenge match was run on Sunday 3 August, when Kitchen's Team raced against Hart's Team. This was followed by another team event on 17 August, when a combined Norwich and Birmingham side took on Middlesbrough.

1947 Roll Of Honour

Shropshire Championship
Andy Mackay

Worcestershire Championship
Reg Lambourne

Nantwich Club Championship
Ralph Ellison

Welsh Championship
Open and 500cc – Graham Parry

Lincolnshire Championship
Harold Caunt

Farleigh Castle Silver Trophy
Dink Philpotts

South-Eastern Centre Championships
250cc – F. Haywood
350cc and Sidecar – Eric Oliver
Individual and 500cc – Bert Roger

Wessex Centre Championships
350cc – Stan Lanfear
Unlimited – Richie Reynolds
Sidecar – Don Slate

Southern Centre Championships
350cc – Bert Croucher
Individual – Dink Philpotts
Team – Southampton

Pontypridd Championship
500cc and Open – Richie Reynolds

Essex Championships
350cc – A.D. Absalom
500cc – Bill Ryan

Scunthorpe & East Midland Centre Championships
Solo – Harold Caunt
Sidecar – J.S.Jenkins/ N.S. Lee

Banbury & Oxfordshire Championship
Jim Wright

Neath Championships
350cc – Eric Davies
500cc – Graham Parry

All-England Championship
Lightweight – Cyril Clisby
Junior (350cc) – Ted Kempson
Solo, Senior and Sidecar – Eric Oliver

Bunkers Hill Championship
Dick Tolley

Eastern Centre Championships
350cc and 500cc – Bill Carruthers
Unlimited – Monty Banks

Oxfordshire Championship
Charlie Wright

Leicestershire Championship
Len Bayliss

OFFICIAL PROGRAMME 6d.

CHALFONTS & AMERSHAM AUTO CLUB

GRASS TRACK

● SPEEDWAY ●

MEETING AT AMERSHAM COMMON, BUCKS

August 31st, 1947   ●   A.C.U. Permit No. Q183

Held under the General Competition Rules of the A.C.U.

OFFICIALS

A.C.U. Steward	TO BE APPOINTED
ub Steward	J. BEDFORD
ie k of the Cours ...	A H. BOWERS
ir ekeeper	H. F. GLAZEBROOK
Starter	H. CHANDLER
Chief Marshal	E. HILL
Paddock Marshal	W. BAILEY
Scrutineer	W. BAILEY, Jnr.
Secretary of the Meeting ...	C. W. KEEN
Press and Announcing ...	D. A. GLADWELL

ST. JOHN AMBULANCE

APPROX. LENGTH OF TRACK 300 YDS.   EACH RACE 4 LAPS.

═ WARNING ═
MOTOR RACING IS DANGEROUS!

You are present at this Meeting entirely at your own risk, and the ticket of admission is issued subject to the condition that all persons having any connection with the promotion and/or organisation and/or conduct of the Meeting, including the owners of the land and drivers and owners of the vehicles and passengers on the vehicles, are absolved from all liability in respect of personal injury (whether fatal or otherwise) to you or damage to your property howsoever caused. **The track is well roped for your own safety. Keep outside the rope.**

BETTING IS PROHIBITED

Amersham programme, 1947.

18
GRASS-TRACK RACING
1948

The golden age of grass-track continued as Farleigh Castle recorded an attendance of 10,000 spectators. Elsewhere, crowds flocked to the post-war circuits all over Britain, including Brands Hatch in Kent and Rocky Park in Cornwall, where all the top names were in regular competition. Meanwhile, at the YMCA Sports Ground, Belvoir Drive, Aylestone, the Leicester Query Club recorded a crowd of 6,000 to watch Len Bayliss win the 350cc, Unlimited and Six Fastest finals.

The South Liverpool Club ran a meeting on the outskirts of the city, at Fazackerley Sports Ground, which saw Ralph Ellison and Bob Parker dominate the proceedings with two final wins apiece. King's Norton in the Midlands brought early season victories for Don Evans (350cc and 500cc), Ralph Ellison (Unlimited and Invitation) and Pip Harris (Sidecar). A new name appeared in the programme at this meeting, namely Vic Artus, who was to later scale the heights of sidecar fame. In this particular meeting at King's Norton, Vic finished second in the Solo Invitation final, and third in the Unlimited Solo final. Vic was, of course, the father of 1970s British Sidecar Champion, Alan.

Ralph Ellison was certainly in form: having won two finals at King's Norton, he also won events at the Nantwich & District Motor Club's event at St Joseph's in Cheshire. The St Joseph's circuit was situated in a field belonging to a theological college, and was an alternative to their regular venue at Birchall Moss Farm in Hatherton.

The Birchall Moss venue featured an off-track start at the pit gate, while the track was some 600 yards in length, on a slight gradient. It wasn't quite mountain grass-track terrain, but after the start, going up the hill there was a jump, and the riders would aviate slightly. The top bend had a full-bore sweep to it, while the back straight featured a slight right-hand kink, and then the riders would fly through the air again, as they met the jump coming down.

The Nantwich Club had been famous for providing the competitors with hot meals and a bottomless tea urn. However, in the mid-1940s, it was decided to do away with the hot meals, although a packed lunch was provided instead. Despite the end of hot food, the tea urn remained in place, so it wasn't all bad for the riders!

Also in the north west area, Harry Terretta won four main finals at the Wirral Club's event, which was staged at Ellesmere Port. Terretta went on to share the honours with Don Evans and Jack Wilkinson in a meeting at Crewe, where another rider going well was Ernie Wood.

The aforementioned Ellison, Terretta, Evans and Wilkinson, along with Harold Stacey and Andy Mackay, starred at Bangor-on-Sea, Wrexham and at Rhyl. Ralph Ellison was triumphant in the Harold Dodd Trophy Race at Bangor, while Ernie Wood was a winner of the same trophy when it was raced for later in the season at Wrexham. Further down

Kingsdown programme, 1948.

OFFICIAL PROGRAMME — SIXPENCE

BRITISH RED CROSS (Wiltshire Branch)

assisted by

HIGHWORTH M.C. & L.C. CLUB

FINAL CHAMPIONSHIP GRASS TRACK MEETING

(Open to Wessex Centre A.C.U.)

Held under Permit No. 179 and subject to the General Competition Rules of the Auto Cycle Union including Racing Regulations Appendix M

at

KINGSDOWN, Near SWINDON

(by kind permission of Mr. W. Denley)

on **SUNDAY, 3rd OCTOBER, 1948**

First Race 2.30 p.m.

OFFICIALS

Stewards:

F. E. B. FELLOWES, Esq. and T. TEASDALE, Esq. (appointed by the Wessex Centre A.C.U.)

J. HUGHES, Esq. (appointed by the Organising Club)

Judge Timekeeper and Handicapper: E. D. CHINN, Esq.

Announcer: D. P. LEAVER, Esq., of Bristol

Starters: L. F. COCKHEAD, Esq.; A. PORTER, Esq.

Recorder: W. RAYNER, Esq.

Machine Examiner: H. JARMAN, Esq.

Paddock Marshals: K. K. WISE (Chief), W. G. CUNNINGHAME, Esq & MEMBERS OF THE HIGHWORTH M.C.C.

Track Marshals: H. TREMBLIN (Chief) & MEMBERS OF THE HIGHWORTH M.C.C.

Parking Marshals: SWINDON & DISTRICT M.C.C.

Programme Marshal: J. PORTER, Esq.

Clerk of the Course and Secretary of the Meeting:

REG. F. J. WISE, Esq., 52, GODDARD AVENUE, SWINDON

The Red Cross Ambulance (Wilts 19 & 21) is in attendance by kind permission of the Officers Commanding

PROCEEDS FOR THE NEW AMBULANCE FUND

PRINTED BY THE SWINDON PRESS LTD., NEWSPAPER HOUSE, SWINDON.

in Shropshire, Don Evans won the Sykes Trophy at Oswestry on Whit Monday.

Talking of Whit Monday, it was certainly a day to remember in Cornwall for Devon rider Ken Slee, when he defeated speedway superstar Jack Parker at Rocky Park, St Austell. Sadly, this was the final season of racing at the Cornish venue, as the following year, the action was to move to the shale, when St Austell opened a speedway track at Par Moor. As well as Parker, many other famous speedway names raced at Rocky Park, both in the pre-war and post-war periods. The star names that appeared in 1948 included Lloyd 'Cowboy' Goffe, Pete Lansdale, Jim Boyd, Bill Pitcher, Cyril Roger and Cyril Quick.

The last-ever meeting at the Cornish circuit was staged on Saturday 14 August, but it was a tragedy for former Cornish Champion Bob Collins from nearby Probus, who sadly lost his life in a track crash. The accident happened in race six, after he had actually won the first heat of the evening. It was, most certainly, the end of an era at Rocky Park in more ways than one.

Speedway riders Eric Chitty and Mike Erskine, of West Ham and Wimbledon respectively, were booked to appear at the Camborne, Redruth & District Motor-Cycle and Light Car Club event at Treswithian in Camborne. Neither of the speedway aces appeared at the head of the results, though, with Cyril Quick topping the individual scorechart on 15 points. The runner-up position went to Ivan Kessell (14 points), with Vic Gent, Adrian Kessell and Des Tamblyn next in line, with 10 points apiece.

The other Cornish venue that saw the top speedway riders appearing on the grass was the Bodmin & District Motor Club's circuit at Racecourse Farm in Bodmin. Meanwhile, there was further grass-track action at Coswarth Farm in Newquay, which was organized by Newquay & District Motor-Cycle and Light Car Club.

Moving across the border into Devon, grass-track racing was also held at the home of Plymouth Speedway, when a meeting took place at Pennycross Stadium, Peverell on Saturday 3 April. Further up to the northern part of Devon, the West of England Motor Club ran a meeting at Exeter on 14 July. The event was held in aid of the Pinhoe Community Centre Permanent Site Fund. Lloyd Goffe was victorious in the Gallows Open final, while Roger Wise cleaned up in the rest of the programme, winning the

ROAD RACING · GRASS TRACK RACING · TRIALS · SCRAMBLES & SPEEDWAY REPORTS

The MOTOR CYCLIST

INCORPORATING THE CLUBMAN'S GAZETTE

| Vol. 2. | No. 3 | May 8th. 1948 | EVERY Fortnight | SIXPENCE |

R. T. PRITCHARD (350 Triumph) and W. D. TURTON (350 Jap) in close company at Warstock. Reported on page 8

The Motorcyclist *magazine, 8 May 1948.*

Grasstrack and Speedway *magazine, 29 May 1948.*

D.A. Brewer and W.K. Parker, pictured at Falfield.

Exeter Open final, the Devon Open final and the Champions final.

Two weeks later, the West of England Motor Club held another meeting at Exeter on 29 July, and Wise was again in superlative form, winning the Devon Open final, the Exeter Open final, the Champions final and the Match Race against Ron Clarke. There were two other finals at this meeting and these were won by John Uglow (Standard Machine) and Ron Clarke (Gallows Open). Incidentally, local Devon rider John Uglow was still racing in the year 2001, when he appeared in a sidecar at the 'Days of Glory' event in Nailsworth.

Gloucestershire was still a popular area for racing, and one event that took place was organized by the Dursley Motor-Cycle and Light Car Club at Green Farm, Falfield on the main Bristol to Gloucester road. The meeting was held in aid of the Stone Village Hall Fund and featured an all-star line-up that included Stan Rea, Bill Davies, Graham Parry, Vic Worlock, Richie Reynolds, Bill Hopkins, Jim Cashmore, Pat Waterman and Reg Lambourne. There were four separate events, with the winners being Parry, Reynolds, Lambourne and Hopkins. Following the meeting, the R.A. Lister Silver Prize Band played in the marquee as everyone danced the night away.

On the outskirts of Gloucester, the Staverton Racing Club held a unique event at their Bamfurlong Farm venue, when England took on Wales in a seventeen-heat team match. The oval circuit was a small one, measuring just 320 yards, but the English boys adapted well to win the match by 68 points to 32, with a side that included Jim Cashmore and Bob Jones. The Welsh squad also featured some well-known names, with Freddie Williams, Roy Zeal, Chris Boss (later to star with Bristol Speedway) and Herbie Jones on board.

Later in the year, Staverton staged a feast of racing with a meeting that included a twenty-heat Individual Championship, a three-heat Best Pairs event and a Fastest Riders final. The pairs event was for novices and was won by Les Taylor and John Hitchings, whilst Reg Lambourne won the Fastest Riders final. Richie Reynolds took the glory in the Individual Championship, scoring 15 points, with Jim Cashmore finishing as runner-up on 12 points. The remaining scores were: H. Beaumont (11), D. Hurn (11), Don Colwell (11), Reg Lambourne (11), Bob Jones (10), John Hitchings (8), Rees Lewis (7), Ernie Baker (6), Bill Downton (6) and Les Parker (6).

Bill Davies, of Shipston-on-Stour, enjoyed his finest hour on 7 August 1948, when he won the Leicestershire Championship against a top-class field that included Harold Caunt, Peter Orpwood, Arthur Sweby, Reg Lambourne and Vic Holcroft. Second place in the final went to Jim Cashmore, while Arthur Sweby finished in third position. The event, staged at The Oval, Abbey Park, during the City of Leicester Festival week, saw Bill not only win the Championship final, but also the 500cc final and both of his heats. Bill, in fact, had a fifty-year racing career that began with a win at a local flower show in 1933 on a Douglas, and finished with a win at a sandtrack in 1983.

Another talking point of the year was the visit of Kent Club Sidcup to the West Wilts venue of Farleigh Castle. The visitors came away with a victory by 36 points to 34, in a twelve-heat challenge match, but you could say, looking at the riders' points, that the inclusion of Roger Wise was a trump card as he recorded 8 points for Sidcup. The full list of scorers was:

Norman Parker and Mike Erskine, pictured in 1948.

CHALFONTS & AMERSHAM
A.C.

Official
Programme 6d.

GRASS TRACK
CHAMPIONSHIP
Meeting

START
2.30 p.m.

A.C.U.
Permit
No. Q 269

T.T.C.
No. 492

At
CHALFONT ST. GILES
SEPT. 26th, 1948

Held under the General Competition Rules of the A.C.U.

OFFICIALS

A.C.U. Steward	F. R. REEVES
Club Steward	J. BEDFORD
Clerk of the Course ...	A. H. BOWERS
Timekeeper ...	T. H. WALTON
Starter	C. W. KEEN
Chief Marshal	D. JACKMAN
Paddock Marshal	B. DIBLEY
Scrutineer	L. FLACK
Secretary of the Meeting ...	C. W. KEEN
Press and Announcing ...	D. A. GLADWELL
Judge	J. BURROWS

ST. JOHN AMBULANCE

APPROX. LENGTH OF TRACK 320 YDS. EACH RACE 4 LAPS.

WARNING
MOTOR RACING IS DANGEROUS!

You are present at this Meeting entirely at your own risk, and the ticket of admission is issued subject to the condition that all persons having any connection with the promotion and/or organisation and/or conduct of the Meeting, including the owners of the land and drivers and owners of the vehicles and passengers on the vehicles, are absolved from all liability in respect of personal injury (whether fatal or otherwise) to you or damage to your property howsoever caused. The track is well roped for your own safety. Keep outside the rope.
ALL CARS TO BE KEPT 10 FT. BEHIND ROPES AT TRACK SIDE.

BETTING IS PROHIBITED

Chalfont St Giles programme, 1948.

Wingfield Park programme, 1948.

Shepton Mallet programme, 1948.

West Wilts – Stan Appleby (8), Graham Parry (6), Dink Philpotts (5), E. Davis (5), Ken Wiggins (4), Tommy Bounds (3), Dick Bradley (2) and Jack Plowright (1) Sidcup – Wally Lock (9), Roger Wise (8), Jack Surtees (6), H.J. Donovan (5), V.H. Harper (4), Ted Kempson (2), D.A. Simpson (1) and G.H. Taylor (1)

It is interesting to note that the points were gleaned from a combination of Solo races and Sidecar races.

The Southern Centre Championships were held at Little Ann Bridge Farm in Andover, and were organized by the Southern Centre A.C.U. The Individual Solo title went to a rider who was to become a legend, namely Freddie Williams, who would later win the World Speedway Championship at Wembley in both 1950 and 1953. Finishing behind Freddie in the Individual Championship was Dink Philpotts, while Don Philpotts was third. It was a memorable event for Williams, as he also defeated Dink Philpotts to triumph in the Experts Solo Championship. In the 250cc final, the winner was A. Smith, while the 350cc final saw Ralph Steere take the title ahead of Jimmy Squibb. Other winners were Stan Appleby (Sidecar), W. Wild (Novice) and Mike Lane (Intermediate). This was the very same Mike Lane who went on to take a record number of Southern Centre Sidecar titles in the 1950s.

One of the year's other major events was the Wessex Centre Championship, which moved to Doulting, Shepton Mallett and was held on 5 September. The Open Championship went to Bristol's Graham Parry, with the Sidecar title going to Stan Appleby. The 350cc Championship also went to another Bristol rider in Stan Lanfear. Rostrum results were:

350cc final – First: Stan Lanfear (Rudge), Second: Pat Waterman (PWS), Third: Roger Wise (Jap)
Individual final – First: Graham Parry (Rudge), Second: Dick Bradley (Jap), Third: Cyril Quick (Excelsior)
Sidecar final – First: Stan Appleby (Norton), Second: Reg Lewis (Velo), Third: Ted Summers (Ariel).

Organised by  Permit No. P14/2

Programme of Events

GRASS TRACK RACING

BRANDS HATCH ESTATE

SUNDAY, JULY 18th, 1948

START 1.30 p.m.

OFFICIALS

Stewards : W. Bournes, A. Yates & one appointed by A.C.U.

Judge : B. Tyler   Starter :

Machine Examiners : B. Peacock, W. Peacock

Timekeepers : D. S. Wallis, W. Harre

Paddock Marshals : A. E. Ridley, F. Neal

Chief Marshal : P. Nicholls

Clerk of the Course : R. Banks

Secretary of the Meeting :

D. S. Wallis, Committee Room, Brands Hatch Pavilion.

Held under G.C.R. of The A.C.U., S. E. Centre.   T/Track Cert. No. 500.

Official Programme :: 6d.

Brands Hatch programme, 1948.

In other areas, racing was held in Ireland at Raheny Trotting Track, Dublin, and in south Wales, several places staged meetings, including Cardiff, Treorchy, Swansea, Port Talbot and Tynycoed Field in Pontardulais. Star names in Wales were Norman Treseder Snr and Norman Treseder Jnr, both from Swansea, as well as Dan Thomas (Maesteg), Windy Rees (Pontardulais) and V. Brinkworth (Pontypridd).

At Treorchy, racing was held at The Oval, and was organized by the Rhondda Motor Club on Bank Holiday Monday 2 August. The list of competitors included Chris Boss (Barry), Roy Zeal (Newport), Richie Reynolds (Worcester) and the Williams brothers (Freddie and Ian) from Port Talbot. Winner of the Novice Solo event at this meeting was H. Wharton from Pontypridd, who was mounted on a 350cc Velocette.

At the Pontypridd & District Motor-Cycle Club event, also in August, Dan Thomas was the top scorer at 350cc level, whist Roy Zeal was the top man on the 500cc machines. Other racing in Wales was organized by the Pontllanfraith Auto Club, Neath Motor Club, Carmarthen Motor-Cycle and Light Car Club and Cardiff Motor-Cycle and Light Car Club, with the latter running meetings at Ely Racecourse.

The Neath Championships this year, were held on 28 August, with the main results being:

Stars at a Wessex Centre event. From left to right: Dick Bradley, Vic Worlock, Pat Waterman, Dink Philpotts, Graham Parry and Bonny Good.

Chesterfield programme, 1948.

500cc final – First: Harold Caunt (HEC), Second: Herbie Jones (Jap), Third: Dan Thomas (OWL)

350cc final – First: Pat Waterman (PWS), Second: Eric Davies (Velo), Third: Chris Boss (AJS)

Points Championship – First: Panther Hurn (Jap), Equal Second: Pat Waterman (PWS) and Graham Parry (Jap)

On the outskirts of Swansea, at Fforest-fach Stadium, racing was staged on a regular basis, with the Treseders and the Williams families often in the thick of the action. This venue nearly became a home to speedway in the late 1990s, indeed, the Stadium is still there and would be ideal for the famous shale sport.

The weather was kind, and another large crowd was in attendance for the annual South-Eastern Centre Championships, organized by the Eltham & District Motor-Cycle Club at Brands Hatch. Don Gray, mounted on his Gray Special, won the Individual title from F. Wood (Velo) and Harry Ditchburn in an average speed of 56.91mph. Other victories at the major event went to Wally Lock (350cc), Cyril Clisby (250cc) and Jack Surtees (Sidecar). The year also saw the formation of the South-East Centre Riders' Association, which would look after the interests of competitors in the area.

In the Wessex Centre, apart from the venue at Doulting (Shepton Mallett) where the Centre Championships were held, several other circuits were utilized, including Bath & West (at Grittleton and also at Rainbow Wood Farm, Claverton Down, Bath), Frome (The Mount), West Wilts (Farleigh Castle), Highworth (Kingsdown), Bristol Combined Motor Clubs (Wallscourt Farm, Filton) and the Douglas Motor Cycle Club (Swinford, near Bitton, Bristol).

Cheshire Centre Champions for the year were Ernie Wood (250cc) and Don Evans (350cc and Unlimited), with the team award going to Nantwich, whose team boasted Don Evans, Ralph Ellison and Vic Masefield. The Shropshire Championships were held by the Salop Club at Lower Edgebold, and saw Len Bayliss triumph mounted on an Ellbee, while Don Evans was the runner-up, with Andy Mackay finishing third.

Jim Cashmore was presented with the Alderman Lunt Cup and Adams Trophy after winning three finals at the Union Auto Club's meeting at Stourbridge Grammer School

Farleigh Castle programme, 1948.

playing fields in Worcestershire. Over in Warwickshire, the Leamington Club presented Roger Wise with the President Cup. This was awarded to the rider with the best performance over the course of the season on a pointscoring basis, with the top three being Wise (56 points), F. Bass (51) and Jim Cashmore (50).

Staying in Warwickshire, the Alcester & District Motor-Cycle Club ran meetings at Aston Cantlow, which was situated three miles from Alcester. The oval circuit was 500 yards in length and the smooth surface featured a slight elevation from one end to the other. Moving into Worcestershire, the West Midland Racing Group had a venue at Hanbury, near Droitwich. The track there was smooth and flat, but was shaped like a heart.

The big event in the Midlands was the Worcestershire Championship, of course, and this took place at the Old Racecourse in Defford Road, Pershore on 8 August. The setting was a large flat meadow and Coventry's Len Bayliss took to it like a duck to water, following up his Shropshire Championship victory with another success. Don Evans was second, while Peter Orpwood had to settle for third position on the podium, but it all went wrong for pre-final favourite Roger Wise, who suffered a puncture and had to retire. It was very frustrating for Roger, as he had won his semi-final and set the fastest time of the day, although he did have the satisfaction of taking the 500cc and Unlimited finals. Don Evans gained some compensation for his defeat in the Championship by winning the 350cc final, while Cyril Smith and Bill Boddice took a Sidecar final win each.

The year saw grass-track speedway held at the Palace Recreation Grounds in Hamilton, Scotland. Also known as the Hamilton Showground, the only event was staged on 15 May and was run in the form of a challenge match which pitched Hamilton

Vic Worlock leading Fred Hill at Falfield.

DURSLEY MOTOR CYCLE AND LIGHT CAR CLUB.

Affiliated to the Western Centre ACU

MOTOR CYCLE GRASS TRACK RACING

Held under the General Competition and Appendix M Racing Regulations of the A.C.U.   Permit No L 408

Saturday June 19th 1948

At Green Farm, Falfield,

On the Bristol - Gloucester Main Road

IN AID OF THE STONE VILLAGE HALL FUND

At 3.30 p.m sharp

OFFICIALS

A.C.U. Steward	J. S. Ashmead
Club Stewards	L. Cohen and L. V. Jones
Judges	F. A. Power and A. Giles
Clerk of the Course and Competition Secretary	N. W. Darby
Timekeeper	A. J. Morris
Starters	J. H. Warner and M. Talboys
Machine Examiner	J. Phillips
Pit Marshalls	A. F. Wyatt, D. Robinson, A. Court and F. Spende
Chief Course Marshall	H. I. H. Simmonds
Chief Public Marshall	D. Davis
Public Announcer	A. T. O'Meara
Honrary Medical Officer	Dr D. C. Prowse
First Aid Personnel	by St Johns Ambulance

NOTICE

The Public are earnestly requested to enter and leave by the official gates only, and to avoid damage to hedges, etc.   They are reminded that they must not, under any circumstances encroach upon the marked Course which is roped for your safety.   The safety of everyone depends upon strict observance of these regulations.

Falfield programme, 1948.

BRISTOL COMBINED MOTOR CLUBS

Grass Track Racing

(Open to Wessex Centre A.C.U.)

Held under Open to Centre Permit No. M.157 and subject to the General Competition Rules of the A.C.U. including Racing Regulations Appendix M

at

WALLSCOURT FARM, FILTON, BRISTOL

(by kind permission of Mr. J. Windell)

on

SUNDAY, 20th JUNE, 1948.

First Race 3.0 p.m.

Officials :—

A.C.U. Stewards - -	C. H. King, F. E. B. Fellowes
Club Steward - - -	- G. H. C. Millington
A.C.U. Timekeeper and Judge - -	V. C. Anstice
Starters - - - -	- A. G. and D. Latty
Machine Examiners - -	- D. Harrison and H. Fowler
Paddock Marshal - - -	- L. R. Parsons
Chief Marshal - - -	- A. W. Burnard
Gate Stewards - -	- R. Soloman and J. Bates
Programme Marshal - -	- T. L. A. Teasdale
Radio Announcer - - -	- D. Leaver
Medical Officer - - -	- Dr. J. E. S. Hamilton
First Aid - - -	- St. John Ambulance Brigade
Clerk of the Course - -	- - C. A. Dickins
Secretary of the Meeting - -	- T. Teasdale

FORTHCOMING EVENTS—WESSEX CENTRE

June 27th—Highworth   July 3rd—Douglas   July 4th—Frome
July 11th—West Wilts—(Farleigh)   July 18th—Shepton Mallet

FLAGS

Yellow—Last Lap   Chequered—Finish
Light Blue—Caution   Red—Stop

OFFICIAL PROGRAMME—PRICE SIXPENCE

Mason & Son, Bristol

Filton programme, 1948.

Graham Parry (1), Reg Lambourne (11) and Richie Reynolds (4) leave the start at Falfield.

Rocky Park programme, 1948.

against the Rest of Glasgow. An individual tournament was also run on the same day and saw Norman Lindsay take victory in the Hamilton Speedway Cup. The meeting formed part of the annual Lanarkshire Farmers Society Agricultural Show, and proved to be popular, with similar speedway style events being held every year until 1955, with the exception of 1952. The riders' dressing room was a large tent, while the pits were located in a sheep pen! The track was bladed out of a grass football pitch and looked comparatively smooth, however, the length is not recorded, as the size probably varied from year to year. A safety fence was constructed of wire netting pinned on to stakes, but there was no starting gate, with car headlights used to start the races.

During the year, racing was also seen at Grimsby (Grove Farm, Waltham), Yiewsley (Stockley Sports Stadium), Sutton Falcons (Sutton-in-Ashfield), Wirral 100 Motor Club (Ellesmere Port), Rotherham (Wickersley), Tenderden (Sandy Lane), Chalfont & Amersham Auto Club (Little Missenden), Southall (London), Ilford (Abridge), Great Yarmouth, Kenton & Kingsbury Motor-Cycle Club (Horsley, Surrey), Moseley (Lowsonford), Chester, Surrey Hills Motor Club (Witley), Worthing, Broughton & Bretton, Ilkeston, Horsham, Castle Colchester and Yeo Vale (Yeovil).

1948 Roll Of Honour

Wessex Centre Championships
350cc – Stan Lanfear
Unlimited – Graham Parry
Sidecar – Archie Appleby

Southern Centre Championships
350cc – Ralph Steere
Solo – Freddie Williams
Team – Southampton

Leicestershire Championship
Bill Davies

Cheshire Centre Championships
250cc – Ernie Wood
350cc and Unlimited – Don Evans
Team – Nantwich

Shropshire Championship
Len Bayliss

Worcestershire Championship
Len Bayliss

Lincolnshire Championship
Harold Caunt

South-Eastern Centre Championships
250cc – Cyril Clisby
350cc – Wally Lock
Individual – Don Gray
Sidecar – Jack Surtees

Neath Championships
Individual – W. Hurn
350cc – Pat Waterman
500cc – Harold Caunt
Neath Stakes – Gordon Parry

Gwent Championship
Roger Wise

Boscombe Championship
Bonny Good

South Midlands Centre Championships
250cc – W. Austin
350cc And 1,000cc W. Kinnear
Team – Wycombe

Highnorth Championship
Fred Williams

Hereford Challenge Trophy
Bruce Semmens

Newcastle Davison Trophy
Alec Grant

Roke Down Championship
Dink Philpotts

Top, middle and bottom: racing at Fforest-fach Stadium in 1948.

19
GRASS-TRACK RACING
1949

A crowd of over 7,550 turned out to watch the racing at a new venue near Bridgnorth in April. The new track at Swancote saw Dick Tolley win the 500cc and Unlimited finals, while Don Evans won the 350cc Class and Pip Harris collected a Sidecar double. Evans and Harris certainly started off well in the Midlands, as they had previously cleaned up at the first meeting of the year in the area, when they took victories at Warstock, which was now the home of the King's Norton Club.

This was another bumper year in the Wessex Centre, with Farleigh Castle attracting an attendance of 10,000 for the opening meeting, while later in the year playing host to a side from London at their grand final event on 11 September. At the Highworth group meetings, a total of £9,000 was raised for charities, with a total of 35,000 people watching the five events staged. A further three successful meetings were also staged at the popular Doulting circuit, near Shepton Mallet.

The Wessex Centre Championships were held on 4 September at St Algar's Farm, near Frome. In the Sidecar event, the title went to Eddie Summers and passenger Cecil Sexton, who were mounted on a Norton. Eddie had previously received major press attention, when he raced a machine that was powered by a motor-boat engine in 1947. John Dore, mounted on a Velocette, won the 350cc event, but it was Bonny Good from Devizes who took the 500cc title. Sadly, Bonny was later to receive some severe injuries in a road accident, which was to end a racing career that only lasted four full seasons. Bonny's career was short but sweet, though, and he also proved to be the fastest rider at the old Blackmore Vale circuit at Cannfield.

Podium results from the Wessex Centre Championships were as follows:

Individual 1000cc Championship – First: Bonny Good (Jap), Second: Danny Malone (Jap), Third: Graham Parry (Rudge)
350cc final – First: John Dore (Velocette), Second: Lew Coffin (Jap), Third: Artie Thick (Jap)
Sidecar final – First: Eddie Summers (Norton), Second: Reg Lewis (Velocette), Third: Tommy Bounds (BSA).

Before leaving the Wessex Centre, mention must be made of the Highworth Group, which was made up of the Swindon and Highworth Clubs. They ran at Kingsdown, on the outskirts of Swindon, and at the last meeting of the season, speedway ace Jack Parker came and presented the Kingsdown Championship trophies to Archie and Tom Appleby (Sidecar), Dick Bradley (Senior Champion), Maurice Leonard (Intermediate Champion) and Henry Burdon (Junior Champion).

Bere Regis programme, 1949.

Bournemouth Motor Club
(Affiliated to Southern Centre A.C.U.)

●

MOTOR CYCLE GRASS TRACK RACES ★ ★ ★

OPEN TO SOUTHERN CENTRE A.C.U.

Held under Permit No. U61 and Subject to the General Competition Rules of the Auto Cycle Union

Roke Down - Bere Regis
DORSET
By Kind Permission of T. V. Snow, Esq.

On Sunday, April 17th, 1949 at 2.30 p.m.

In Aid of Bere Regis British Legion

OFFICIALS

Stewards	A. E. Lambert, Esq. (Southern Centre A.C.U.)
	G. W. Bennett, Esq. (Bournemouth M C.)
Starter	W. H. Scullard, Esq.
Starter's Marshalls	E. S. Hiscock, Esq., J. Beasley, Esq.
Timekeeper and Judge	L. W. Avery, Esq.
Lap Scorer	J. Gilson, Esq.
Machine Examiner	J. Couling, Esq.
Pit Stewards	Messrs. L. Trowbridge, J. Coombs, J. Dominey, R. White
Track Marshalls	Members of the Bournemouth Motor Club
Programme Sellers	Lady Members of the Bournemouth Motor Club
Ambulance	Dorchester Division of St. John Ambulance Brigade
Clerk of the Course and Secretary of the Meeting	J. Bowater, Esq.

Official Programme, 6d.

There was no chance of a rider taking both the Wessex and Southern Centre titles, as they were both held on the same day! Organized by the Bournemouth Club, the Southern Centre's big event was staged at Roke Down, Bere Regis. The Individual 1,000cc title was won by Bingley Cree, who had been a pioneer of grass racing in the south, having started racing at the age of fifteen. Bingley was aged thirty-five when he won this major event, but much earlier in his career, in 1935, he had finished as runner-up. It was a great day for Cree, as he also recorded the fastest time of the day at the 1949 Championships, on his way to victory over Bob Oakley and Tony Lewis. The other results from the big event were as follows:

250cc final – First: Arthur Harris, Second: R. Stillo, Third: R. Hancock
350cc final – First: Dink Philpotts, Second: G. Ames, Third: Stan Formhalls
1,000cc Novice – First: D. Hayles, Second: Dave Lane, Third: S. Dean
1,000cc Non-Expert – First: Tony Lewis, Second: J. Cleave, Third: J. Countley
1,000cc Expert – First: Bingley Cree, Second: Bob Oakley, Third: Dink Philpotts
Sidecar final – First: George Buttigieg
Team – First: Bournemouth (48 points); Second: Ringwood (46), Third: Southampton (44).

Bob Oakley, who had to take second best to Bingley Cree in the Centre Championships, was the Southampton Speedway captain. During the season, Bob had the opportunity to present the 1949 Aston Combine Championship Trophy to up-and-coming grass-track and speedway ace Jimmy Squibb.

Grass-track racing was about to go into decline in the 1950s, before picking up again in the 1960s, but there was still plenty about in the south, west and Wales areas during 1949. Meetings could be found at Hereford (King's Acre Road), Worcester, Gloucester, Cardiff, Newport, Newbridge, Pontypool, Aberaman, Southampton and Burford.

Unfortunately, in the south-east, it was the final year of the great circuit at Brands

Tense moments for Bonny Good, Dick Bradley and Bob Jones.

Grass aces line up for the camera, including Dink Philpotts on machine and Bonny Good at his left shoulder.

OFFICIAL PROGRAMME — SIXPENCE

THE R.A.F. ASSOCIATION

Assisted by

HIGHWORTH M.C. & L.C. CLUB

GRASS TRACK MEETING

(Open to Wessex Centre A.C.U.)

Held under Permit No. M75 and subject to the General Competition
Rules of the Auto Cycle Union including Racing Regulations
Appendix M

at

KINGSDOWN, NEAR SWINDON

(by kind permission of Mr. W. Denley) on

SUNDAY, 28TH AUGUST, 1949

First Race 2.30 p.m.

OFFICIALS

Stewards:

V. O. KEELING, Esq. (appointed by the Wessex Centre A.C.U.)
J. HUGHES, Esq. (appointed by the Organising Clubs)

Judge Timekeeper and Handicapper: E. D. CHINN, Esq. (A.C.U.)

Announcer: D. P. LEAVER, Esq., of Bristol

Starters: L. F. COCKHEAD, Esq.; A. PORTER, Esq.

Recorder: W. RAYNER, Esq.

Machine Examiner: H. JARMAN, Esq.

Paddock Marshals: K. K. WISE (Chief), W. G. CUNINGHAME, Esq.
& MEMBERS OF THE HIGHWORTH M.C.C.

Track Marshals: H. TREMBLIN (Chief) & MEMBERS OF THE
HIGHWORTH M.C.C.

Parking Marshals:
SWINDON & DISTRICT M.C.C. and MINETY VALE M.C.

Programme Marshal: J. PORTER, Esq.

Clerk of the Course and Secretary of the Meeting:
REG. F. J. WISE, Esq., 52, GODDARD AVENUE, SWINDON

The Red Cross Ambulance (Wilts 19 & 21) is in attendance by
kind permission of the Officers Commanding

PROCEEDS TO "BATTLE OF BRITAIN"
WEEK

PRINTED BY THE SWINDON PRESS LTD., NEWSPAPER HOUSE, SWINDON.

Kingsdown programme, 1949.

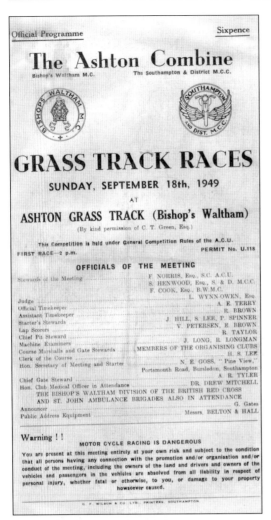

Bishop's Waltham programme, 1949.

Hatch, but although it was to be grass-track's loss, it would become road racing's gain and hold many fantastic meetings in the years that lay ahead. The South-Eastern Centre still produced some of the top competitors, with the Individual award for the year going to Don Whitbread, who was a member of the Sidcup Club and raced a 499cc Rudge machine. Second place went to Bill Keel (JAH Triumph), while Dave Spain (Jap) finished in third position. The first three in the Sidecar event were all mounted on Norton equipment, with Les Taylor winning from G.E. Harris and H.J. Butler. Meanwhile, Tom Turk (Turk Special) took victory in the 350cc final, ahead of Wally Lock (OM Special) and Dave Spain (Jap).

The other major event of the year was the Eastern Centre Championships, which saw Peter Ferbrache (Hartley Ariel) take the 650cc final. The runner-up position went to W.R. Ryan (WR Special), with P. Jefferies (Douglas) finishing in third place. In the 350cc final, Bill Merrett (Velocette) emerged victorious, ahead of I. Radcliffe (Triumph) and J. Steel (Ariel).

It was another year of plentiful race action, which included events at Lincoln, Southall, Newport, Worcester, Wrexham, Rhonda Valley, Leicester, Dublin, Leatherhead, Pontypridd, Pontypool, Cardiff, Peterborough, Aberman, King's Norton, Nantwich, Whitley, Leamington, Horsham, Rochester, Oswestry, Runcorn, Ilford, Barry, Manchester, Grantham, Luton, Folkestone and Newcastle.

Sadly, it was a fond farewell to Brands Hatch, but the superb venue left many magic memories. In October, a record attendance of 18,000 watched the end of racing at a track which had hosted grass-track racing over a seventeen-year period. Centre Champion Don Whitbread finished in style when averaging 59.23mph to win the Brands Hatch Championship. Also at the final meeting, Tom Turk won the 350cc final, averaging 56.63mph, while Phil Seymour won the Sidecar event. All-time lap records at the Kent circuit were recorded thus: Cyril Roger (Solo) 60.39mph and Phil Seymour (Sidecar) 53.19mph.

Wessex Centre champion Bonny Good, pictured with his awards.

Dick Bradley, wearing his Bristol speedway race jacket.

157

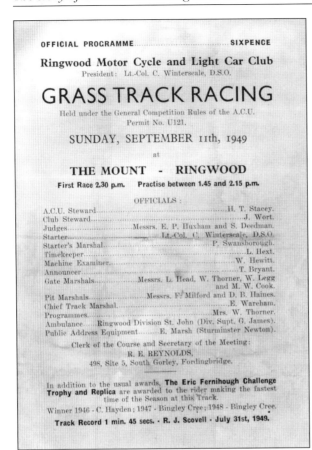

OFFICIAL PROGRAMME..................SIXPENCE

Ringwood Motor Cycle and Light Car Club
President: Lt.-Col. C. Winterseale, D.S.O.

GRASS TRACK RACING
Held under the General Competition Rules of the A.C.U.
Permit No. U121.

SUNDAY, SEPTEMBER 11th, 1949
at

THE MOUNT - RINGWOOD
First Race 2.30 p.m.   Practise between 1.45 and 2.15 p.m.

OFFICIALS :

A.C.U. Steward.................................H. T. Stacey.
Club Steward....................................J. Wort.
Judges................Messrs. E. P. Huxham and S. Deedman.
Starter.............................Lt.-Col. C. Winterseale, D.S.O.
Starter's Marshal..............................P. Swansborough.
Timekeeper.....................................L. Hext.
Machine Examiner................................W. Hewitt.
Announcer......................................T. Bryant.
Gate Marshals............Messrs. L. Head, W. Thorner, W. Legg
and M. W. Cook.
Pit Marshals...........Messrs. F. Milford and D. B. Haines.
Chief Track Marshal.............................E. Wareham.
Programmes.....................................Mrs. W. Thorner.
Ambulance......Ringwood Division St. John (Div. Supt. G. James).
Public Address Equipment........E. Marsh (Sturminster Newton).

Clerk of the Course and Secretary of the Meeting:
R. E. REYNOLDS,
498, Site 5, South Gorley, Fordingbridge.

In addition to the usual awards, **The Eric Fernihough Challenge Trophy and Replica** are awarded to the rider making the fastest time of the Season at this Track.
Winner 1946 - C. Hayden; 1947 - Bingley Cree; 1948 - Bingley Cree.

Track Record 1 min. 45 secs. · R. J. Scovell · July 31st, 1949.

Ringwood programme, 1949.

Another classic championship, which actually started in 1932 and is still going strong in the new millennium, again took place in 1949, namely the Worcestershire Championship. This saw future National Champion Dick Tolley put his name on the trophy, after winning the ten-lap final from runner-up Reg Lambourne, and third-placed E.G. Rees. Dick also won the 500cc (from Reg Lambourne and J. Pain) and Unlimited finals (from Len Bayliss and Reg Lambourne), but could only manage third place in the 350cc final, behind winner Reg Lambourne and second-placed Len Bayliss. Cyril Smith took the flag in the 600cc Sidecar event, with G. Bretherick finishing second, and Sid Hall third. In the Unlimited Sidecar race, it was G. Bretherick who emerged triumphant, ahead of Cyril Smith and the, again, third-placed Sid Hall.

1949 Roll Of Honour

Wessex Centre Championships
350cc – John Dore
Unlimited – Bonny Good
Sidecar – Eddie Summers

Southern Centre Championships
250cc – Arthur Harris
350cc – Dink Philpotts
Individual – Bingley Cree
Sidecar – George Buttigieg
Club – Bournemouth

Kingsdown Championships
Solo – Dick Bradley
Sidecar – Archie Appleby

South-Eastern Centre Championships
250cc – Bill Keel
350cc – Tom Turk
Individual – Don Whitbread
Sidecar – Les Taylor

Worcestershire Championship
Dick Tolley

Welsh Championships
Solo – Ian Williams
Sidecar – Reg Lewis

Eastern Centre Championships
250cc – R. Allen
350cc – Bill Merrett
650cc – Peter Ferbrache

Neath & Carmarthen Championships
350cc – Ted Evans
500cc – Chris Boss

Folkestone Championship
Cyril Roger

Aston Combine Championship
Jimmy Squibb

NEWBURY & DISTRICT MOTOR CLUB

GRASS TRACK
MOTOR CYCLE
MEETING

Grand
Championship
MATCH

TOMMY PRICE'S CUP

AT

SANDLEFORD FARM, NEWTOWN ROAD, NEWBURY

(by kind permission of Mr. S. Butler)

SUNDAY, AUGUST 7th, 1949

First Race—3 p.m.

Held under the General Rules A.C.U. South Eastern Centre

Permit No. P.216

◆◆◆◆

LIST OF OFFICIALS :

Secretary of the Meeting } Clerk of the Course }	C. Bennett
Stewards	R. Smith, P. Mallin, C. Nicholls
Official Starter	S. A. Simmons
Paddock Marshals	R. Wilson, J. Eastman, W. Wakefield
Announcer	J. Olive
Timekeeper	T. Smith
Machine Examiner	R. Wilson

OFFICIAL PROGRAMME

BLACKET TURNER & CO. LTD., PRINTERS.

Newbury programme, 1949.